IN THE
COMPANY
OF
FAIRIES

IN THE COMPANY OF FAIRIES

An Unconventional Memoir

LORI L. SWEET

LIONSCAPE PUBLISHING

First Edition 2026
Print Book Interior design and typeset by Lori L. Sweet
Cover Design © by Lori L. Sweet
Cover Photograph by Taichi Nakamura via Unsplash
Interior Images Designed by Freepik, used with permission

ISBNS: Paperback 979-8-9948422-1-8
Library of Congress Control Number: 2026907733

LionScape Publishing
Harrisburg, Pa
Printed in the United States of America
LionScape Publishing is an Imprint of Lori Sweet Studios

www.LionScapePublishing.com

CONTENTS

Storytellers are descended from an ancient and immense community — made up of holy people, wounded people, visionaries, healers, artists, and the so-called "crazy ones" who carried the stories when there was nothing else to carry.

~ Clarissa Pinkola Estés
(adapted from Women Who Run With the Wolves)

Dedication

To all who delight in nature's beauty, mystery, and wonder. To all who ponder the strange, the inexplicable, the numinous.

PART 1:

ENTERING THE LANDSCAPE

I remember a moment when I decided that whether or not the world was magic, it was better to live in it as though it were.

~ Caroline W. Casey

THE HEARTFELT TRUTH

*Someday you will be old enough to start reading
fairy tales again.*

~ C.S. Lewis

I t was a profound episode in my life. There was no way I
could have anticipated the peculiar and unexpected events
that unfolded on the morning of March 13, 1995, along Belleview
Road, nor what followed in the months afterward. Thirty years
later, the memory, still lingering, has continued to weave itself
through the fabric of my life in ways both subtle and profound.

My twenties were somewhat turbulent and difficult. I'd
had a challenging divorce, a new baby with medical needs, and
financial worries, but after turning thirty-one in February, I
felt like things were looking up. As I took a walk that March
morning, I was wondering what this next decade of my life
would bring with hopeful anticipation.

That ordinary walk, however, was about to take an extraordinary turn. What was about to happen would open a door

I didn't know was there. It was a door into another world ~ a door into the realm of fairies. It has taken me three decades to write that sentence wholeheartedly and to share it openly, as its deeper influences and personal meanings have gradually revealed themselves to me.

For reasons I can't fully explain, my life has long been intertwined with the the mysterious and the otherworldly. These experiences have appeared throughout my life, often rooted in nature, sometimes even before I had the language or context to understand them. At times, that disorientation led me on a quest for meaning and deeper understanding. At other times, I had to accept what could not be known or proven.

In retrospect, I can see how this ongoing relationship with the mystical realms and the inner life has allowed me to serve as a bridge between the worlds, between the seen and unseen. I believe it is not only possible but important to live with both a grounded practicality and a deep trust in our second sight and intuitive sense.

Many of us, as children and adults, have had moments, even if fleeting, when we sense something otherworldly: a presence in the room, a message in the wind, a synchronicity, a premonition, a visitation. Perhaps you've had such experiences. These unusual encounters often arrive unannounced, shimmering through the mundane, reminding us the veil between worlds might be thinner than our culture would like us to believe.

Such things, whatever they are, always have been part of the human landscape. That alone fascinates me. Whether literal or symbolic, real or imagined, I believe these experiences matter. They matter even if all we can do is share our stories and ponder the possibilities. They speak to the intricacies of a complex living world and the depths yet to be discovered and understood by humans.

While this is a deeply personal and true-life account, I offer it not just as an isolated story but as mythopoetic witness, a voice in a universal choir, a story within stories that invites you, the reader, into your own meaning-making of the mystical and the mysterious.

CHARTING THE TALE

~ Carson McCullers

This memoir reveals experiences that took place in my life over a five-month period in 1995. I have presented the events as faithfully as my journals from that time and my memory allow.

It is told through a creative framework, a narrative lens, that emerged organically when I first began writing about this period in my life. The story unfolds as a nested narrative set within a fictional cottage, told through the voices of two symbolic storytellers, Alma and Kaiah, a grandmother and granddaughter. They serve as extensions of my own voice. The result is an unconventional memoir that seeks to convey the relational depth and spirit of what occurred.

As an orientation to the book, let me briefly walk through the sections. Part I guides you to the doorway and invites you to enter. (You are here now.) Part II holds the story itself. Part III contains my personal reflections on the story. Part IV is a place to pause where readers can reflect on the story alone or with a group. Part V expands the view, offering an introduction into the realm of fairy lore and origin stories. A resources section follows.

Together, these sections trace not only what happened in 1995 but also how the writing of this story took root in my heart and my life. It has become a life-spanning conversation with a mystery that continues to this day.

PART 11:

THE TELLING

Stories are medicine. They have such power; they do not require that we do, be, act anything ~ we need only listen.

~ Clarissas Pinkola Esté

"Everything you can
imagine is real."
~ Pablo Picasso

PROLOGUE: KAIAH BEGINS

My name is Kaiah and I want to share a story with you. It is something my grandma, my Alma, entrusted to me when I was only ten years old. I vividly remember Alma telling me her story. Some experiences, some stories, have that kind of effect. They work their way into your psyche and wrap around your heart for a lifetime. As I reflect on that time, as the adult I am now, I see it from a new perspective.

Time has worked its own magic.

I've come to understand why my Alma always said such stories need to be shared in a respectful way and at the right time. Stories, like all living things, need fresh air and space to grow. The time feels right to share her story again.

This is how I remember it.

I

THE ARRIVAL

I arrived at my grandma's cottage on a sunny Friday afternoon prepared to spend the weekend with her. Alma was celebrating her 62nd birthday on Sunday and the rest of the family would be coming. But until then, it was just the two of us.

Alma, the name I lovingly use to address my grandma, wasn't her given name. It was simply the name that came to me as a small child, and it stuck.

That evening, Alma made us a pot of soup with fresh tomatoes, zucchini, and carrots along with homemade sourdough bread and chocolate pudding for dessert. The sweet aromas filled the air as the oven warmed the cottage.

While we ate dinner, Alma asked me about school and friends. We talked and laughed. As the sun began to set in streaks of pinks and yellows over the trees in the far lot, she pointed out the window and reminded me how to tell the difference between the oaks and maples, beech and aspen. She told me that learning the names of our neighbors is important. She said trees were like friends.

We cleaned up the dinner dishes, mostly in silence, in the slow and deliberate way my Alma did it. She even took time to carefully fold the empty bread bag and tuck it away for reuse. She talked about how small acts of kindness, such as recycling, add up to help our planet.

The cool evening breeze made us close the windows. I could hear the crickets and fading birdsong outside. Alma brought in some extra wood and then made herself a cup of tea. She gave me some fresh lemonade. It was a favorite of mine.

Finally, we began getting comfortable around the fire. A familiar sense of anticipation was building. Alma told me earlier she'd be sharing a story, a true story, she said, one I hadn't heard yet. It was a story close to her heart, she had confided. By that time, I'd already been listening to grandma's stories for a long time. I loved our story times.

Thinking back, I can recall my dad, Alma's son, often smiling knowingly at his mother's stories. He appreciated her eccentric ways, while my mom just rolled her eyes and called Alma's stories *tall tales*. Alma would kindly huff at them both, wave her hand as if to dismiss them, and laugh.

Alma loved telling stories and I loved hearing them. She told me tales from around the world and other cultures, myths and fables, and spooky stories, too. She liked some of the classics, like *The Chronicles of Narnia* or *Snow White*, but what she loved most was to tell stories about nature.

Sometimes she told me old folk tales like "How the Zebra Got Its Stripes," but she also taught me things like how storm clouds form, how plants communicate with each other, and how honeybees dance.

I still hear her saying, "We *have to see with soft eyes and listen with our inner ears to understand the language of things.*" She told me that all good relationships require time, attention, respect, and love. Being in relationship with the earth, and the beings of the earth, was no different.

When I was younger, I believed all my grandma's stories were true. Then, for a while, I wondered if maybe Mom was right about some of them being tall-tales, like her stories about UFOs and ghosts. Now I realize that Alma saw some kind of truth in every story she told.

She was a story-weaver who could see between the worlds. Like myths and fables of old, complex truths were spun in the telling. She would say there are different ways to listen to a story. Listening with the heart was most important.

Alma had a way of sharing things she deeply cared about that made it clear there was more to our world than meets the eye. She wasn't flighty, and she never spoke from a place of whimsy or fantasy. Her words, grounded and sincere, carried weight, not because they could be proven, but because they came from a truth deep in her bones and out of her lived experience. She often said that truth isn't just something you read in a book or prove scientifically. "Truth, *the bigger truth*," she claimed, "is...well, bigger."

The fire crackled loudly as Alma poked it with her stick and red sparks flew up the chimney. I knew she was about to start when she turned to me and smiled. Her face was illuminated by the flames as she softly spoke, "Kaiah, honey, do you need a blanket?"

I answered with a nod of my head, and she handed me a soft, full-sized, blue and green quilt she had hand-stitched herself. I snuggled under the warmth of it as I sat attentively in a big brown chair. I always felt safe in Alma's presence, as if the world outside didn't matter when we were together. She had a way of making everything feel okay, even when life was uncertain.

Alma cleared her throat and with her usual air of story-telling formality, asked, "Would you like me to tell you a story?"

I looked up at her with a smile as I exuberantly responded, "Yes!"

She leaned back in her chair grinning at my enthusiasm. And without further delay, she began.

"Many years ago," she said, "I lived in a little town called Bemus Point in Western New York. I recently had rented a little red house on a private piece of land overlooking Lake Chautauqua. It was a special little place, magical in its own right.

"The little red house has its own story, one I will share with you some other day," she teased, "... but this story, the story I want to tell you tonight, actually began on a Sunday morning, on March 13th, thirty years ago, when I decided to venture out from my little red house and take a walk to a nearby woods."

Alma hesitated, gazing up and back down, as if choosing her words carefully, then continued. "Something happened to me that day. Something I'll never forget. Kaiah, as you know, unusual and mysterious things weren't new to me, yet this encounter, this visitation, well, it was the kind of thing that changed how I saw the world. It asked something of me and yet it gifted me with so much more."

Even then, I knew this about my grandma. She often talked about psychic and supernatural experiences, lucid dreams, and intuitive insights. This just seemed to be who she was. She lived life tuned into the unseen and hidden worlds around us and within us. I could tell her about my unusual and strange things, too. I think everyone has them.

Once, I was dreaming about being in a cave with bats flying all around me. When I woke up, I felt something brush my face and realized there were two real bats flying in my bedroom! My dad put them outside in the morning, but the next night they were back, tapping on my window from outside. I was certain the bats were trying to tell me something.

Alma always took me seriously when I told her about such things. She let me know that sometimes things happen we can't explain, but we still can have fun exploring what they might mean to us. We've always had fun talking about our adventures.

That night, long ago, in the comfort of her little cottage, was no exception. Curled up in my chair with a full belly and an open heart, I excitedly encouraged her, "So...what *did* happen to you on March 13th?"

With a shyness I seldom saw on Alma's face, she looked down for a moment, then raised only her eyes to look up at me over her glasses and said, "Well, on that morning, two fairies appeared to me."

2

A NEW BEGINNING

As soon as Alma said '*two fairies appeared*,' I blurted out, "Alllmmmaaaa," and giggled. "Mom says fairies aren't real! I thought you said this was a true story!"

Now, as an adult looking back, I realize I may not have been very sensitive to the tender reveal my grandmother had just shared with me. My ten-year-old self couldn't help but giggle. But inside I was wishing that what she said was true!

She paused with a patient sigh, as she did sometimes, leaned forward, and, with a teasing but serious look, said in her deepest voice, "I might be getting ahead of myself. Let's start again. Do you want to hear the story or not?" Then she winked with a half-smile.

I sheepishly nodded, rolled my eyes, and whispered, "Yes, please."

Reaching up to secure a clip in her hair, Alma took a deep breath and began again. "I just had turned thirty-one years old in February that year. It was a special birthday for me and that may have been because it came after a particularly difficult time in my life. I was learning that life doesn't always work out the way we plan. At the same time, I was learning how to grow from adversity, how to forgive, and how to love and find joy despite pain and disappointment."

Making a clicking noise with her mouth, like a sound of regret, my grandma shook her head as if to give pause in honor of the problems she'd overcome. I didn't know all the details then, but now, as an adult, I know more about the struggles she faced when she was younger.

There were the challenges of her first marriage, the demands of raising a child with medical needs on her own, and a career in social work that exposed her to the abuses and struggles inherent in our world.

I've also had the privilege of reading some of her personal journals that helped me to better understand what she had endured. In 1989 she focused on her efforts to *fit in* and *be normal.*

She wrote,

> *I have become a stranger to the natural world. I miss playing in the woods like I did as a child. When did I stop? I have given up my dreams and creative ideas to focus on work and home and marriage. I guess it makes the family happy. It is the way of the world. But why don't I feel happy? I feel very sad and far away from myself.*

There came a time when my grandmother realized she was denying her true self, closing off the very things that made her feel alive and vibrant. Something inside of her was crying for help.

Alma once told me about the day she walked out of her kitchen door during a moment of clarity and self-awareness. She lay down in the grass until the full moon came up that night. As a matter of fact, she slept outside all night on a lounge chair. That night changed her life. Although her husband, my grandfather, thought she was crazy for sleeping outside, she said she felt saner than she had in a long time.

In her journal she wrote,

> As I laid on the ground and touched the earth, I could feel it breathing with me. As the sky darkened and the stars came out, I could feel the whole universe breathing. It was as if life itself was being breathed back into me. I remember now, as a child, how I felt so at peace in nature, in wild places. Oh, how I long for that sanctuary again.

I believe that night began a journey for her back to nature, back to herself, back to life. But, now, on this night, as Alma began telling me her story about the fairies, she didn't share the depths of her sorrows or the extent of her healing journey. Maybe she thought I was too young to understand back then. And probably, I was. So, instead, she only briefly referenced that time in her life, made that clicking noise, and paused for a moment before she resumed her story.

Alma looked like she was trying to choose her words carefully as she continued.

"By the time my thirty-first birthday arrived, things had started to calm down. Moving into the red house in Bemus Point along Route 430 felt like a fresh start, a place of healing. At first I thought it was the house. But it wasn't. It was the land. I didn't understand that right away. From the front porch you could see Lake Chautauqua. It felt like sacred ground.

"I was longing to renew the deep childhood connection I once had with the earth and instinctively knew it would soothe my weary body and spirit. Moving into this house and turning thirty-one felt like a time for recovery and new beginnings.

"Out there, looking over the lake at night, with all those stars... it felt like the rest of the world couldn't reach me. I needed a refuge, a safe place. I didn't have words for it then, but I felt like I belonged to that land."

Alma quickly raised her arm above her head and we both looked up to the ceiling. Her gesture was to help me imagine the sky as she spoke.

"That morning in March, so long ago, the sky was bright blue," she said, "an unusual occurrence at that time of year in Western New York. The sun shone brilliantly in a refreshing way and the hint of spring was in the soft cool breeze.

"The birds, oh, they were singing, calling, celebrating. I'd been studying wild plants and birds for several months and was feeling proud of myself because I could identify by sound and sight the cardinals, blue jays, robins, sparrows, and wrens in their morning concert. Their songs were so real and crisp in the early rush of life."

She looked across the room as if she could see the birds and then looked down and waved her hand over the floor describing the earth below.

"Winter's barren mark still could be seen across the land, but greening grass and small patches of crocus and daffodils caught my eye as I walked. The road behind my house was Belleview Road, a quiet country back road. I saw no people and no cars that morning as I walked, yet the world felt vibrantly alive."

As Alma shared her story, I realized all my life she'd been teaching me the songs of birds as well as the names of plants and trees. I never asked her where she learned it all herself. *Who taught her?*

I tried for a moment to imagine Grandma as a young woman walking alone in the morning sun, listening joyfully to birdsong. Then I remembered she mentioned seeing fairies, and I felt excited trying to imagine where this story was headed.

3

IN PRAISE OF NATURE

I brought my attention back to Alma's voice as she began speaking again.

"The area was rural, but it was speckled with old farms and lake cottages. I was walking toward a familiar wooded area with a narrow creek running through it. For the past six months, ever since I moved into the little red house, I frequently visited this patch of forest to sit quietly, write, draw, or take a nap. I'd walk along the creek, a tributary of the Chadakoin River, and think about how long it had been there. Long before me. Long before any of us.

"When I reached the path into the woods, I paused before stepping off the road. I offered the remains of the apple I was eating to the spirits of the woods by placing the apple on a rotting stump and asked the trees for permission to enter."

"Wait," I said, stopping Alma mid-story.

Again, I was struck by the thought that Alma hadn't always been *Grandma*. She had a life before now, full of experiences I'd never really considered. It was odd to think of my grandma as a younger person, and I tried to imagine her as a woman with a life of her own – before mine.

My curiosity grew and I asked, "Even back then, you were talking to trees?'"

She just smiled and said, "Yep. Even back then."

Then she asked, "Shall I go on?"

"Yes, please," I said. And so she did.

"A crow flew overhead," she said, as she moved her hands like a bird for effect. "It sharply called out as it swooped into the trees above me – Caw! Caw! I took that as a sign of welcome and stepped onto the dew-covered ground still littered with old leaves and dried twigs from last fall.

"I was headed to that creek, my usual spot, but after only a few steps, I found myself drawn to a specific tree I'd never noticed before. Something about it held my attention. Looking back now, I believe I was in a mild trance or altered state. The tree seemed strangely inviting, and I was drawn to walk over and touch it.

"That day, instead of continuing to the creek, I spread my blanket out next to this tree. I arranged myself so I could lean my back against it and sit facing the morning sun. After I got situated, I sat quietly and said a morning prayer. It was something I had learned years before from a Seneca elder."

When Alma said *Seneca elder*, I was pretty sure I knew the prayer she referred to. It began, "*Oh Great Spirit, I awake, to the rising sun ....*" She'd tell me later she learned it from Grandmother Twylah Nitsch of the Seneca Wolf Clan. I was trying to remember more of the words when I noticed she was staring at me. She put her finger to her lips and spoke in a hushed tone.

"When I finished with the prayer, the woods... they became, well, ...strangely... quiet."

The fire crackled suddenly as a spark flew out from the flames, and we both jumped! Alma stood up and put out the spark with her foot, brushing it back onto the stone floor. She started talking again even before she returned to her chair.

"So, as I was saying, on that morning, there was this unnatural silence that raised the hair on my arms. I no longer could hear the birds, the wind, or the creek. I felt as if something had changed although everything looked the same. The world was so quiet..., I wondered if I literally had gone... *deaf*. I started to panic a little."

Alma held her hands up to cover her ears and I imitated her.

"It's amazing," she said, "how many thoughts you can have when it's that quiet. It feels like time is standing still."

I'm sure my eyes were as big as saucers, and I was sitting right on the edge of the chair holding my breath. Alma audibly exhaled so I could exhale too. I wondered if it really was possible for time to stand still? Can people suddenly go deaf? Before I was able to ask any of those questions, Alma went on with her story.

"I started to feel... calmly... alert... and emotional," she said. "The trees were speaking to me without words. I somehow *understood* the trees were lonely or sad. Something was wrong."

Alma sighed deeply. Her tone shifted again, as if she were speaking to herself.

"I'm starting to notice how often the things that happen in our lives are like threads, connecting the past and the present, weaving it all together. Just now, as I was talking about the trees, a vivid memory came back to me about another time trees communicated with me. I hadn't made this connection before."

She paused.

This is how my grandma often tells stories. She goes off on tangents. Stories within stories. I wasn't sure what my grandma meant exactly, but I could imagine threads being woven together, so I nodded as if I understood.

Then I asked, "So, what did you remember?"

She clapped her hands together as if she was pleased I'd asked.

"Well, I'm reminded of a time in my life when my family was on vacation in the Adirondack Mountains. I was just a little girl, just about your age, Kaiah!

"In spite of the fact we were on vacation, on a sunny day, and all seemed right with the world, I began to feel a growing sense of agitation. My heart was pounding and my throat tightened as we drove up the mountain. I didn't know what was happening to me.

"As I paid more attention to the sensations in my own body, it became clear to me the trees were crying, though I couldn't explain how I knew this. It was as if they were speaking to me in an unspoken language, something transmitted rather than heard. It was an unfamiliar and unsettling feeling. I didn't yet understand why they were grieving, but I was about to find out.

"When we reached our destination, the reason revealed itself. Acres of trees on that beautiful mountain had been cut down recently to make way for a large parking lot at the entrance to an amusement park called Santa's Workshop, in none other than North Pole, New York. I felt certain the trees were experiencing grief over what they probably considered a tragedy.

"My parents didn't believe me when I told them what I thought and felt. They were not amused by my dramatic display of concern nor when I told them I didn't want to go into the amusement park. I was accused of imagining things and ruining the family fun. It upset me at the time, but I don't blame them. What could they make of it?

"Later, I wrote down my experience in a journal I had taken with me. I wanted to honor the trees somehow. Writing it down would ensure I wouldn't forget them. I also collected a small piece of bark from one of the trees that day. It was a paper birch tree that stood near the edge of the parking lot. I still have it in a scrapbook."

"Wait, Alma, you have the tree bark?" I inquired with interest as I sat up straight.

"Yes," she said as she reached around to a low bookshelf near her chair and pulled out an old scrapbook that was falling apart. She opened it to a page where there was a piece of tree bark taped to the yellowing paper. I reached over and touched it.

Alma shifted in her seat to regain her focus. Then she snapped the scrapbook closed. She waved her hand in front of her eyes as if to wipe away the images of the experience she was describing and brush it away.

She sighed, looking off into the distance and said, "Well, that is a whole other story in itself. I'm getting off track a bit, aren't I? I guess I told you about it because that experience stayed with me. It helped me to understand how nature communicates with me and how my body senses things in moments that feel... well... beyond the ordinary. It solidified my growing fondness for nature and deepened my respect for living things."

As I listened, I thought about the trees being cut down on such a beautiful mountain. At ten years of age, I already was no stranger to the environmental concerns that plagued our earth. I knew about the damage humans were causing, sometimes out of necessity, sometimes out of disregard. I swallowed hard, feeling butterflies of helplessness in my stomach. But Alma brought my focus back to the story at hand.

She cleared her throat before resuming her story.

"So then, as I sat in the little sunny patch of woods that morning in 1995, I had a similar experience. I had an intuitive sense that the trees were letting me know they were distressed, but there was something more.

"As this uneasy feeling hung in the air, I wondered how long it had been since anyone had cared for these trees. I was glad I'd been coming to visit this seemingly forgotten little patch of woodland for several months by then. With all that had happened in my life, I had my own grief and loneliness, and I felt like the trees understood. I thought maybe they simply were reflecting my own sadness back to me."

Alma rubbed her hands together and then placed them on her chest. I noticed the soft wrinkles and delicate skin on her hands. I loved her hands.

She continued, "As I sat there, I began to wonder why humanity has grown so indifferent to the world that sustains us? Why do we think we have the right to take more than we need? How do we protect and praise what we love?"

Then she looked at me wide-eyed, bobbing her head, and added, "These are difficult questions to unravel, for sure. In that silence it seemed like I had lots of time to think, but I didn't have answers. My mind was racing only with questions."

As I listened to Alma, my mind was racing with questions, too. I must've looked worried because she patted my hand reassuringly.

She cocked her head and raised her voice in a playful way. "Now, mind you, all of that *thinking* probably took place in a matter of a few seconds. Everything felt suspended in time. It was then I had the visceral sensation and awareness that something was watching me sitting there."

"Oh, no!" I chimed in. "Were you scared?"

"No," she said, shaking her head gently.

"I wasn't afraid. But I was aware of feeling as if I wasn't alone. And I was right."

4

A HIDDEN REALM REVEALED

Alma looked up and pointed across the room as if looking at something. Her voice was dreamy as she described her memories.

"There was a group of three distinct trees standing about fifteen feet in front of me. I thought my eyes were drawn to them as a point of focus, to get my bearings, but then something shifted near the trees. I still couldn't hear anything.

"I began to feel as if the world in front of me was bending. There was a subtle movement in my visual field that made me feel slightly dizzy. I felt a strange tingling sensation down my spine and was oddly fixated on those three trees. Everything was in slow motion. That was when I saw them."

I was holding my breath as I listened to Alma. She squinted her eyes as if to demonstrate looking off into the distance while lightly swirling her hands and fingers around in the air to conjure up the scene.

Then very softly she said, "Two glowing lights emerged from behind the center tree. Or perhaps they came from within the tree. I don't know actually, but it felt as if they *entered* the woods from someplace else. They were, maybe, as large as my open hand or slightly larger. They floated in the air about five or six feet off the ground."

I gasped as Alma described what she saw. I remained quiet with my hands covering my mouth. She continued to motion with her hands and fingers, as if she was weaving invisible threads as she spoke.

"They appeared like flickering light, brighter or denser in the center, fading into soft edges. They seemed to be moving closer and then farther away from me, but I couldn't quite focus my eyes on them to judge the exact distance. The sun shone behind them in soft, broken beams between the leaves. But their light was distinctly different."

I blurted out, "Wow! That is so cool. Did they have wings? What did they look like?"

"Oh no," Alma replied as she wrinkled up her nose, "although they did appear to be flying in some way. I didn't see any wings. I couldn't see any details. One was larger than the other one though."

I listened intently to every word my Alma was saying and felt myself swallow hard when her tone changed.

"Kaiah, do you need to take a break?" she asked. "This is a long story, and we can get some more lemonade if you want to."

"No, no!" I almost yelled, my face twisted in annoyance. I tugged on her sleeve eager to hear more.

"Come on, Alma! Don't tease. What happened next?"

She grinned, a sly twinkle in her eye, as if she knew she was annoying me. After adjusting her shawl around her shoulders, she lowered herself down on the stool, closer to the floor.

I think she was imagining herself sitting by the tree long ago as if it was easier to remember that way. So, I sat next to her and imagined sitting by the tree, too.

I leaned against her and whispered, "Alma, keep going, please."

"Kaiah, it's hard to put it into words exactly. I was mesmerized, you know, in awe. My mind scrambled for an explanation. Could they be moths? Big fireflies? Was it sunlight reflecting on my glasses? I took my glasses off, but the lights remained. I rubbed my eyes and looked again. They remained.

"At the time, it never occurred to me to get up and walk over to them. I'm not sure I could have gotten up even if I had thought of it. As I recall it now, it seemed as if I was transfixed. I wasn't afraid, but I was trying to comprehend what was happening."

She paused, her gaze drifting toward the fireplace, and then in that dreamy tone she said, "While my mind was busy struggling with an explanation, another part of me was fully present, calm, and alert. That part of me simply was observing and witnessing this phenomenon and seemed content to do so.

"The lights were constant, though they seemed to dim and grow brighter as they slightly swayed. I blinked hard, but they remained visible. Then, suddenly, a tingling sensation, like pins and needles, flooded through my body. A great sense of warmth and peace rose up within me. With it came a knowing: *I really was seeing something!* In that moment, I stopped doubting it. I stopped thinking. In that moment, I truly believed two worlds touched."

Alma stretched over with her finger pointing toward me, and I reached over and touched my finger to hers. It was a moment I felt fully seen and loved.

Sitting back, she continued, "With this new sense of certainty, I fully believed that *whatever* I was seeing was alive. The lights were a living thing ~ two living things. As I watched them, I was overcome by a tenderness that erupted within me and brought tears to my eyes. There was a palpable feeling of compassion and beauty that stretched beyond time, something immense and eternal. A sense of humbling appreciation followed that is... I must say, hard to describe, hard to put into words."

She leaned forward and spoke in a whisper.

"As I watched, I heard myself asking myself, '*If they ARE alive, then WHAT are they?*' And, as if in response to my interior question, I immediately heard the answer form in my mind, only they were not my words. The lights answered me.

"'*You would call us fairies,*'" they said.

I interrupted Alma. "Wait. What? They spoke? What did they sound like? Could you see their bodies?"

Alma dropped back in her chair, flopping her arms against the armrests, and said, "Sweetheart, it is hard to say exactly. They didn't speak like we do. It was some kind of telepathy, more like putting words in my mind that were not my own. It was as if I could hear them speaking in my head, and yet it was different than my own thoughts. The woods remained silent. I didn't see any figures, though I sensed their personalities. I only saw the small lights, yet their presence felt much larger in size."

She paused for a moment for effect and to see if I understood. I offered a quiet look of recognition that I was following her every word.

Her voice was laced with a kind of playful anticipation as she explained, "It took me a minute to let their words settle in, but then I had a realization. I thought to myself, 'Oh, my gosh, they ARE *fairies!*'

"And with that, it was as if something opened up inside of me. It was a wonderment! My brain still was struggling to grasp what was happening. Then, somehow, the quiet woods grew even quieter. I had the sensation that I was in a tunnel or looking through a telescope. Everything became even more focused and intensely beautiful."

I could not take my eyes off of Alma. I was holding my breath again. She had me now. Hook... line... and sinker.

5

A VEILED REQUEST

I leaned forward, nearly standing, to catch every word. Alma paused and closed her eyes, perhaps re-living the memory, but I was impatient.

I poked her and whispered, "Alma, please keep telling me the story." Then I flashed her a cheesy grin when she opened her eyes.

She tried to hold back her amusement at my facial expression but couldn't help but laugh. She patted my head then whispered back to me, "Sometimes part of the story is told in the silence between the words. Patience, my dear girl."

I groaned but respected her need for silence and settled back on the floor. While I waited, I imagined the flickering lights and the trees. I wondered what it'd be like if the world were so silent you could hear fairies speak. Alma, still quiet, stood up with great ease to put another log on the fire.

She settled back into her chair. After another minute, she resumed her tale.

"Okay then... where was I? Oh, yes, I had the feeling the lights, the fairies, were trying to communicate with me somehow. My mind kept interrupting, searching for explanations. It made it harder to stay present and listen. Beneath that, I sensed an urgency, as if they were trying to tell me something important, something I couldn't decipher or make out yet.

"At the same time, another part of me was listening. It urged me to stop analyzing, to stop thinking, and to reach out with the only thing I could offer in that moment ~ love and respect. I remember sending love from my heart and simply waiting."

Alma put her hands over her heart and held them there as she spoke.

"I felt a slight pressure around my temples, and I remember telling myself to breathe. I still had some doubt about what I was seeing. I admit that. But something was happening as I watched.

"At times, one of the lights would disappear behind the tree or seem to vanish into it, only to reappear moments later. I somehow knew one was older and one was younger, but they were both adults. The older one carried a masculine presence, the younger one feminine."

Taking another audible breath, Alma paused and rolled up a sleeve on her sweater.

"Even though I had a feeling of concern, I also felt held, seen, trusted. It was peaceful. I don't know how much time passed. I felt as if I were receiving a kind of quiet guidance, more impressions than words. I thought they had risked being seen for a very important reason, a reason I was yet to discover.

"Suddenly, even though they hadn't changed or done anything differently, I felt the unmistakable knowing within myself that it was time for them to leave. A tight knot formed in my belly.

"In my mind, I pleadingly said, No, *not yet*. I didn't want this, whatever *this* was, to end.

"It all felt so real, and I felt so alive. I wasn't ready for them to go. But with calm, polite finality, they let me know they had to leave. They floated for a few more seconds in front of me, and I heard myself say *Goodbye*. A few seconds later, their lights started to dim as they moved toward the tree, then disappeared. They were gone."

Alma's face looked so tender. I reached over and gently touched her arm. She placed her hand over mine, warm and soft. Her eyes sparkled dimly in the fire's glow, but I think they sparkled because she had tears welling up.

"I never saw them again," she said. "I just sat there. I blinked and moved my head as I tried to get the lights to return. But they didn't. I looked around, half-hoping for a flicker, a whisper, anything. I had the sensation of moving backwards.

"I felt a strange mix of confusion and sadness mingled with joy and excitement. I knew something profoundly spectacular had happened, and I was overwhelmed with the urge to cry. I don't know why exactly. It felt like both grief and longing."

Alma stopped then.

We sat there for a few minutes. My mind was spinning so much I couldn't even form a question. I was startled when Alma suddenly and unexpectedly threw up her arms.

She yelled, "All of a sudden, I could HEAR again! The sounds in the woods returned and it was so LOUD!"

We both laughed at her outburst.

Caught up in the excitement of the moment, I leaned into her lap and hugged her. Alma squeezed me tight and spoke faster now with enthusiasm. She was darting her eyes around and pointing again as she explained.

"You see, a squirrel was digging in the leaves a few feet from me to my left. The squirrel was so close to me that I jumped, and my sudden movement startled him. It felt as if I'd just re-materialized from another world, like I'd simply popped back into this one!

"I could hear the water gurgling and the breeze playing in the quaking aspens on the other side of the creek. The birds' singing was so loud it overwhelmed me. Hearing again made me think I must have been somewhere else or somewhere else had been here! The sudden return of sound was strange and undeniable."

I remember telling Alma it must have been an amazing experience. She seemed emotional at this point. She told me that although thirty years had passed, the whole experience was etched in her mind and her body as if it happened yesterday.

It was hard to know what to say, but I had no doubt this was important to her. I got back in my chair and snuggled under the quilt again. Then, with my eternal childhood impatience and a coy smile, I asked, "Sooo...thennn...whaaat...happened next?"

6

THE AFTERMATH

Alma told me she needed a longer break before she continued her story. She wanted to stretch her legs a bit. She got up and walked to the kitchen. I followed her. I sat on a stool as she stood leaning against the counter. As she folded a couple of kitchen towels, she handed me a new pack of napkins to open and put in the napkin holder. Then she started telling me what happened after the fairies disappeared.

"I sat there for a while at the base of the tree in the woods, trying to collect myself. Once I gathered my senses, I immediately sketched what I'd seen and jotted a few notes in my journal, trying to catch the details before they slipped away. I didn't want to forget a single thing.

"I sat wondering why the fairies were there. *Were they fairies? Did they protect the land? Were they lost? Had they always been there? Was I crazy?* I could only speculate."

I reflected to her, "They said they were fairies. They must have been fairies. Right?"

Alma paused as she looked down at her hands, and then said, "Kaiah, honey, what they said to me was *You would call us fairies.* So that is what I call them. As I think back now, I wonder what they called themselves!" Alma exhaled her frustration with a big sigh.

I asked her, "So, what is a fairy?"

Without hesitation, she said, "That is a very good question, and there isn't one clear answer, my dear. It's a bit of a mystery. That day I felt as if they were otherworldly beings embedded in our natural world, in a world of their own, that must normally be invisible to us."

I accepted her answer.

She returned to her story. "When I finally did get up to leave, I didn't feel quite normal. I stumbled out of the woods and got back on the road. I was disoriented a little, like you might feel waking up in the middle of the night and wandering to the bathroom half asleep. As I walked home, I was aware of a child-like feeling of wonder, yet a subtle sense of dread lingered in my body."

It was hard for me to listen without asking questions. I couldn't help it. I had to interrupt Alma again.

"Wait. So, that was it?! You just saw them, and then they were gone?" I huffed, expressing my dissatisfaction with this development. I felt a little let down, and my face must've shown it.

"You just walked home?" I inquired further in my disappointed tone.

We still were standing in the kitchen when, after my questions, Alma shook her head, chuckled, and silently motioned for us to head back to our chairs.

Once seated, she sat forward holding my hands in hers. Her voice was tender as she answered me.

"No, no, little one, don't be frustrated. The story is only beginning. Seeing the lights, the fairies of Belleview Road, well, that was all special, of course. If it were all that had happened, it still would be pretty amazing. What happened after, over the weeks and months that followed... well, that is the rest of the story."

Alma added, "I think the fairies called on me to have faith of some kind. They asked me to believe in something I couldn't see or prove; to believe in something beyond myself and perhaps to risk looking foolish. They asked me to open my mind and heart. I didn't know it yet, but I was given a choice that day."

She sighed, "But I'm getting ahead of myself again."

As I watched my grandma's face, I was having a hard time imagining what the rest of the story could be! I had so many questions. I was getting sleepy and my eyes must've betrayed me because she looked at me in a motherly way and asked, "Are you tired? Sometimes it's easier to listen to a story when you're asleep."

I assured her I was not tired. I fibbed.

Alma looked a bit skeptical but relented.

"Well, okay. I'll tell you a bit more before bedtime but it's getting late. So, just a bit more. Okay?"

I clapped my hands in agreement; happy I could sway her.

Days passed and turned into weeks," Alma began. "Life went on. I went to work, took care of our home, and cared for my son, your dad, who was about four years old at that time."

"It's funny imagining Dad only four years old," I chimed in.

Alma chuckled. "I bet it's hard for you to imagine your dad that way, but he was a baby once. Your dad has had some otherworldly experiences of his own. You should ask him about them sometime."

I didn't know that about my dad. I tucked that bit of information into my memory for later.

"When I think back to those days," Alma said, her voice sounding more inquisitive, "I recall that a part of me wanted to talk about what had happened, but who could I talk to? Who would believe me or understand? I still wanted to know ~ *Why it happened? What did it mean? What was I supposed to do now? Did I imagine it all? What did the fairies want?*"

"I'd have so many questions, too," I said, to comfort my grandma but then I began to ramble with questions. "How did you figure it out? What did you do? Did you find someone to talk to?"

With her eternal patience she said, "Well, I returned to that same spot in the woods a few times hoping to see the lights again, but the area remained unchanged, as if nothing ever happened. I saw and heard nothing more from the fairies. I could feel myself trying to *remember* what they told me that day as if it was buried somewhere in my subconscious. It reminded me of times I've tried to recall a dream that keeps slipping away. I could feel the memory lingering somewhere in my mind, just out of reach."

Alma looked at me gently and asked, "Ever try to catch a dream but it slips away the harder you try?"

I understood completely and said so.

Alma gently yawned and said, "Yep, it happens. Usually, we just let go of the dream, but in this case... whatever it was I was trying to remember would not let go of me, and I knew it."

7

A TIME FOR REST

E ven though I wanted to continue, Alma gave me a look that said otherwise.

"It's been a long day," she said. "Let's go to bed and we'll finish the story in the morning."

"Noooooo, no!" I said, a little frantically, crossing my arms and slouching back in the chair, pouting. "I wanna know what happens next."

But Alma was standing up already, and I knew it was useless to say anything more. I headed to my bedroom as she followed me. I changed my clothes, brushed my teeth, and got into bed. She kissed me.

As I settled in, she turned out the light, and I heard her say, "May your dreams guide you now."

A minute later, I heard the screen door gently open and shut. At first, it was hard to go to sleep because I kept imagining fairies in the woods. But as I lay there, drifting toward sleep, a warm, comforting stillness wrapped itself around me.

The soft creaking of the old house and the faint scent of lavender from the pillow hinted at a promise of safety I couldn't explain back then but deeply felt. The last thing I remembered was imagining Alma standing outside on the front porch with the moonlight shining on her. All felt right with the world. I knew morning would come soon.

When I woke up, I heard the soft patter of rain on the roof. I looked outside to see rain misting from a cloud-covered sky. Although the sun had risen, there was nothing but a blanket of damp gray covering the world.

Alma was making breakfast already. I could smell eggs, toast, and muffins. She turned with a big grin and greeted me as I came into the kitchen.

"Good morning, my little one. How'd you sleep?"

"I slept fine and I'm hungry. Breakfast smells good," I told her.

We ate mostly in comfortable silence and casual conversation. After breakfast we went out on the covered porch. The misty rain still fell, but the air was warm, and it felt good to be outside.

Alma placed her hot cup of tea down carefully on the side table, her eyes twinkling as they met mine.

I could feel the unspoken expectation in the air, my anticipation growing as I waited for her to speak.

8

TEACHINGS OF THE HEART

As I waited, my thoughts lingered on Grandma's story from the night before. I couldn't help but wonder what it must have been like to meet two fairies in the woods. I realized I was utterly captivated by her tale.

I was daydreaming, really wishing I could see fairies, too, when I realized Alma was staring at me. It was as if she could read my mind because she said, "You know, Kaiah, sweetheart, we all have unique experiences in our lives. We can't compare our life to another person's life."

Alma stopped then; her gaze was tender as she looked out at the rain-drenched garden and then back at me.

"My dear," she began again, "I've tried to share the joy and wisdom of nature with you because I believe it's a good teacher. It nourishes us and gives us beauty. But like every relationship, it's a two-way street. We have to show up, like a trusted friend."

I was fidgeting with my napkin, twisting it between my fingers. I met her gaze when she looked at me again. I knew she was right. She'd spent so much time encouraging me to explore the natural world.

I thought back to that morning we'd spent watching the cicada molt with its fragile wings drying in the sunlight. We would've missed it if we hadn't gone for that walk. Or the day we saw baby spiders being born. In fact, we would've missed so many things, so many small wonders, if we hadn't wandered out in nature as often as we did.

I had so many questions. I just picked one. "Do you really think trees and animals know when we love them?"

Alma answered with a question. "What do you think?"

I felt a little shy, but said, "Well, yes, I think they must."

Alma's voice was steady, and her words carried the weight of her years of experience. "All things grow better with love," she said. "Human intelligence is wonderful, but it's not the only kind. Opening ourselves to the natural world invites us into a glorious relationship. Remember, it isn't just about grand moments. The ordinary moments are filled with wonder and magic too, if we pay attention. Remember the two bats you discovered in your room?"

I told her I remembered.

"Well," she affirmed, "that was an ordinary moment when you were paying attention and those bats made your dream come to life in a magical way."

Alma stopped talking then. The soft tapping of rain on the porch roof filled the space of silence now between us. It was an ordinary moment and wonderment was in the air.

Alma sat up, adjusted the pillow behind her back, and added, "You know, Kaiah, in the end, all we can do is love the world and choose when to protect what is dear to us. It doesn't matter if anyone believes us, or understands it, or approves."

Looking back now, I realize there was a sadness in her words, a quiet kind of grief that comes from loving something deeply that others may not value in the same way.

At the time, I knew she was trying to comfort me, but now from my adult perspective, I believe it was something more she planted inside of me. Alma was teaching me about love, loving myself, loving the world, not in a sentimental way, but in a big and honest way. She wanted me to love the life I was living even if it was different from hers or anyone else's. My journey would be my own.

That morning, we sat quietly for a while. The overcast day and the gentle rain seemed to draw the world closer. It was ordinary yet sacred in its simplicity.

I glanced up at Alma and said, "I think I understand, Alma, I do, but it still would be fun to see the fairies like you did."

I covered my face with my hands, feeling silly for my desire. When I looked again, Alma was smiling mischievously and then said something that has stayed with me all these years.

"Oh, but that's why I'm telling you the story, honey. Don't you see? As I tell you the story, you're imagining what I'm describing, aren't you?"

I nodded affirmatively.

Alma continued, "Words are like magic. They allow me to take the thoughts in my mind and translate them into words, and you, Kaiah, take those words and then form images in your own mind, and translate what they mean.

"We have given meaning to the sounds we make and the marks we put on paper, and they enable us to do this incredible thing. As I talk, you can imagine the fairies and they live in you, too. That's magic."

I liked this new idea about words. It made me smile, and I felt the warmth of Grandma's tender wisdom settle in my chest.

As I sat there, lost in her words, I smiled thoughtfully and waited. I felt something deeper, but I didn't have words for it back then. I realize now that the story wasn't just about what happened in the woods. Telling her story was about sharing a part of herself with me.

In telling her story, she was giving me a gift. It was a chance to live in the magic of it with her. The real gift wasn't in the fairies themselves. It was in the telling, in my belief in her, in the way it opened me up to something greater than what I could see alone. It also was the gift of love Alma and I share.

She reassured me, "You're so smart, and I have no doubt you'll get this all sorted out for yourself."

Then she asked, "Hey, it's sort of damp out here. Do you need something to keep warm?"

Without waiting for me to answer, she got up, went inside, and returned with sweaters for both of us. As she helped me slip on my pink sweater, I felt Alma's love wrap around me like a warm embrace. Her words that day would stay with me, quietly shaping how I understand and experience myself in the world, over all these years.

9

A TOUCH OF THE IRISH

After we settled into our seats again, I sat looking at my grandma's face with her glasses resting low on her nose. I noticed her grey hair loosely tied up in a bun, her skin softly wrinkled with life experience. My thoughts trailed off a little. I continued to try imagining her as a woman in her thirties, full of life and wonder, walking in the sun with long, flowing hair, beads braided in, wearing old jeans and a denim jacket.

I envisioned her raising my father when he was little, lost in her thoughts about the fairies. I'd seen pictures of her when she was a young mother, but now, as she told this story, she had summoned that younger version of herself and brought her to life for me.

I soon realized Alma was speaking again. As I brought my attention back, I heard her talking about a local outdoor festival that was happening the summer following her encounter. She was preparing to attend.

Alma was in mid-sentence already.

"... so, I went to this local arts and nature festival on a beautiful day in early June. By then, a couple of months had passed since I saw the fairies. I hadn't thought about the fairies in while. I just wanted to go to the festival on a pretty summer afternoon.

"There were vendors selling jam, artwork, honey, and knitted scarves. There were outdoor music performances and lectures going on. The air buzzed with activity as I walked down a trail, wooed by the sound of a distant guitar.

"But then I heard her voice. It was a woman's voice, clear and rich, floating above all the noise. Everything else faded away. I was drawn to the sound of her words alone, like a magnet.

"Soon I came upon a woman standing on a small wooden stage in a circular grassy area with trees in the background. She wore a green, flowing dress and her reddish hair fell to her shoulders. Her approach was casual, but instructional.

"About thirty people sat scattered on blankets and lawn chairs listening to her speak. They seemed captivated by her words. There was a man with her too, and they both had strong Irish accents. I slowly walked over and sat down on the grass to listen."

Alma cleared her throat as she took a sip of her tea that likely was cool by then. I was imagining the festival but had no idea what was about to take place.

She continued, "My body responded to the woman's voice before my mind could grasp what was happening. I could feel my heart pounding as I tried to absorb her words, the truth of them sinking in. I started to feel a little dizzy as I realized the woman was speaking about the fairy folk of Ireland and about experiences people had with fairies from all around the world.

"As she gave her lecture, a cool sensation swept across my forehead. I had that same narrow, suspended feeling I felt the morning I saw the lights. Everything became very focused. I had one foot in this world and one foot in another. It was hard not to cry."

Alma changed the tone of her voice. She sounded more serious now, more matter of fact, as she looked straight at me, which always captured my full attention, and spoke, "You know, I'd been trying to figure out who to talk to about the fairies. As I sat there in the grass, it occurred to me that maybe this woman was someone I could talk to. I remember thinking to myself, *Who is this woman? Do people in Ireland believe in fairies? Could Fairy Folk be real? Was it possible? Who was I to claim I had met up with a couple of fairies?*

"But here was this woman speaking about them, publicly, no less. Surely, she wouldn't think I was crazy, *right?*"

I was watching Alma intently as she spoke. A lock of her hair had fallen onto her forehead. Her expression was thoughtful. She paused and shifted a bit, drawing her shawl up around her shoulders.

Though delayed, I blurted out, "Right," in response to her question. Alma shook her head as if to clear her thoughts.

Alma looked down and was moving her hands as she spoke. "Once the talk was over, the crowd quickly dispersed, and soon I was alone in the field. The speakers were packing up their belongings. Although I was nervous, I gathered up the courage to approach the woman to ask her if she might have a few minutes to talk with me.

"Without any hesitation, she smiled in an unguarded way and put her arm around me as if we had known each other for years, almost as if she had been expecting me. She motioned to the man to let him know we were taking a walk, and we found a quiet place to sit together. She seemed to be in no hurry.

"When I told her I had a story to share she encouraged me to tell her everything. She sat quietly and listened as I spoke. I told her all about the fairy encounter and shared my worries that I had failed to understand what they were trying to tell me. When I was done, she told me to breathe deeply several times and to close my eyes."

Alma closed her eyes and began taking deep breaths. I watched her and noticed I was holding my breath again, so I started breathing with her.

After a few moments, Alma went on. "As I sat there with my eyes closed, the woman leaned in and softly said, 'They would not have shown themselves to you if you were not capable of understanding them. You DO know what to do. You just need to remember.'

"A wave of relief washed over me then," Alma said. "It was as if all the weight I had carried for weeks suddenly lifted. This woman's words were a healing balm. She validated me. There was no sense of doubt or disbelief in her voice. I felt myself relax.

"The woman took my hands in her hands. A few tears ran down my cheeks even though my eyes were closed. I could feel the sun on my face, just like the morning I saw the fairies. That gentle warmth from the sun seemed to rekindle my memory. All the sounds of the festival faded from my awareness. Everything became quiet inside. Time felt as if it was standing still once again.

"Then, after a few quiet moments passed, the woman said, 'Remember. You know what to do.'

"I felt as if I was outside of my body listening. Words magically rose up into my throat. I heard myself say, '*There is danger there. They want me to move them to a safe place. Not all of them will go, because some will stay behind.*'"

After she shared this, Alma spoke faster. "I opened my eyes, heart pounding, mouth agape, and stared at the woman sitting in front of me. *Who just said that?* The words seemed to have come from somewhere deep within me, yet I had no conscious part in forming them."

I interrupted my grandma. "That is so neat! You knew all along! Right? It's like she helped you remember. Did this woman know what to do next?"

"Well," Alma responded, "the woman speaking with me now had tears in her own eyes and asked me, 'Yes, and how will you do this? How will you move them?'

"Again, an answer came out of my mouth with a strange certainty. '*I am to take the bark from the tree they were near that day. They will be asleep in the bark.*'"

Alma sat back in her chair as if exhausted, and said, "To this day, I have no idea where those words or such an idea came from. But it felt as though the burden I'd been carrying was gone, and in that moment, I finally understood what the fairies had been trying to tell me.

"The woman said, 'That is very good! They must need help and felt they could trust you.'

"At that moment, the absurdity of it hit me. Half laughing and half crying, I muttered, 'Well, exactly *what* am I supposed to do now? Tell everyone I am helping to relocate fairies? That sounds so crazy!'"

Alma made a crazy face and we both laughed.

She continued, "The woman kindly responded as she put her hand on my shoulder. 'Shhhussh, dear,' she said, 'I know it might feel overwhelming right now. It's okay. Sometimes we have to risk looking foolish to do the right thing,' she told me, 'or the true thing or the fantastic thing. Life is full of risks, but risks so often lead to amazing things in life.'

"The woman gently touched my arm in a soothing way to focus my attention and again said, 'I know this might feel overwhelming right now. I think you have been given a gift. You also have been given a choice. You can help them or not. You can choose to walk away in disbelief or believe what you saw and heard even though you can't prove it. You have to decide what path to take. This is your decision. Only you can decide now.'"

"Wow. Alma." was all I could say. I could feel my own heart pounding. I felt happy, though, knowing Alma found someone to help her.

"Wow is right, Kaiah," she replied, "because when the woman finished speaking, I felt a shift in my surroundings. The gentle sounds of the day came back into my range of hearing, and I realized the festival was wrapping up. I took a deep breath. I felt grateful. My time with this woman felt complete.

"I thought I understood what I had to do, so I wiped my tears, thanked the woman, and turned to walk back to my car. About half way up the road I realized I never had asked for the woman's name. I stopped just as I felt the breeze pick up with a cooler air. I turned and ran back down the hill to catch her, but she was no longer anywhere in sight."

IO

A PLAN EMERGES

The wind blew across the porch as I interjected, "I'm glad you found someone to talk to about what happened. That woman sounded so nice. Did you ever find her again?"

"No, dear, I didn't. But it clearly felt like destiny when we met. In the very least, it was perfect timing like some shimmering synchronicity."

"What is synch... synchrisity?" I tried to ask with my ten year old brain.

"Well, synchronicity," Alma pronounced clearly, is when two things happen that are not directly connected but appear to relate to each other in some symbolic or significant way. It's like a nudge from the universe... being guided by divine and creative forces. You feel it matters and you need to pay attention to it."

I silently was trying to grasp her meaning when she added, "Oh, we can use the example of your bats again. After dreaming about bats you woke up and saw real bats in your room. It was a synchronicity, because you felt like it meant something more than a simple coincidence."

"Hmm," I said, "I get that, I think."

Alma tried again. "Or remember the day you were curious about turtles and we talked about them for a while?"

I remembered. I also remembered that Alma and I had seen a wild turtle on our walk later that same day. The next day in school our teacher seemed to randomly share a story about a turtle. All of this led to me getting my own pet turtle, which I adored.

Alma said, "These little synchronicities seem to guide us, inspire us, excite us, enliven us. They are like little signs that ask us to pay attention, even if only to engage more fully in life, like you did by getting a pet turtle and caring for it. If we follow them, one thing leads to another, and they come to matter in our lives."

I thought I now understood what Alma meant by synchronicity, so I continued my questioning. "Do you believe other people see fairies, too?"

"It seems so," Alma said, nodding. "There are stories all around the world about fairies and other such beings. When a story shows up again and again over time and across cultures, it suggests it's rooted in some kind of truth, or at least a shared understanding that touches the human heart and spirit in meaningful ways."

My whole body felt warm and tingly as I listened.

My grandmother pointed to a stack of books beside her chair and told me she'd been doing more reading on fairies recently. I picked up one of the books and opened it. There were lots of drawings of fairies inside. Alma shared some of what she'd been learning.

"Fairies," she explained, "are said to be magical beings found in many old European stories. Some were kind and helpful, while others were tricky, dangerous, even life-threatening. They looked and behaved sort of like humans."

I looked up at her. "Like humans? You mean big like us? What about fairies like Tinkerbell? I thought fairies were small and had wings. Are there different kinds of fairies?"

"There may well be different kinds, Kaiah." Alma grinned. "You've probably heard about fairies as tiny, winged beings, but they come in many sizes. You're right to be curious about that. You ask very good questions."

She went on. "No one knows for certain what fairies are. But their stories have been told for a very long time."

I closed the book on my lap and placed it back on the pile.

"It'd be fun to read some of these books together," I said, "but I want to know what happened with YOUR fairies, Alma. Did you decide to help them? What did you do?"

Lifting a hand to her chin for second, she said, "Very well. Where was I?"

"Oh, yes. I was trying to figure out what to do with the information I'd gathered at the festival. It was a lot to process. I still wasn't sure what my next steps should be. It was then I had the idea to talk with my friend, Jason."

"Jason? Who was Jason?" I asked. I wasn't familiar with that name.

"Jason was a new person in my life that summer," Alma explained.

She told me a mutual friend had introduced them several weeks earlier. Jason was a free spirit and deep thinker. She felt he was someone she could trust, even though she didn't know him well, and followed her impulse to share her story with him. Alma's voice hinted at the relief she must've felt to talk to someone else about what she'd experienced. She always says the right people seem to show up at the right time. I can see now it was part of the synchronicity she spoke about.

Alma explained, "As I revealed the whole ordeal to Jason, he listened patiently. Then, without hesitation or judgment, he said, 'Just do it. So *what* if it wasn't real? So *what* if you are crazy? So *what* if you spend a few days of your life believing in fairies enough to help them? What is your alternative? What if you don't do it and they are real? Can you live with that?'

Alma grabbed her stomach as if she had just gotten punched. "His clear and simple questions hit me right in the gut." she said. "*What if?* ~ that was a good question. What if I was only afraid of looking silly in a world that often seems too suspicious and callous for such things? What if I didn't believe it and I was wrong? *Could I live with that?*

"I decided I would rather spend my time doing something that possibly could help the fairies, whatever they were, than ignore them. I realized if I didn't do it, I probably would waste my time doing nothing much anyway. *How would I feel if I didn't do it? What would it mean if I did?*

"I had lots of questions but, in the end, I began to look at it as an adventure I didn't want to miss. And an adventure is exactly what it turned out to be."

When I remember Alma like this, I realize just how much I love hearing about her adventures, especially this one. I know my life has been richer because of my Alma. She has helped me to see things from perspectives that've made life more awe-inspiring.

She always makes me feel like life is an adventure. If we pay attention to the things we love, we may discover unexpected treasures. She still inspires me, and now I see all the gifts of her story-weaving more clearly.

Alma resumed her story. "Once I decided I was willing to help the fairies, I had to figure out exactly how to do it and where to take them. This process took three days. I thought about all the wild places I knew in the area and about the state parks and national forests. But nothing seemed like the *right place.*

"I made a trip down to the wooded area where I had seen the two lights to see if I could glean some insight. The woods felt ordinary so I just sat there for a long time. I think I even nodded off for a while.

"Then, as my mind was drifting, I felt something I only can describe as an inner nudge. They were thoughts that were not my thoughts. It was like remembering a forgotten dream. It was magical. A plan was taking shape in my mind. I was getting instructions even though I saw no fairy that day, and before long, I knew what I had to do!

"I *knew* I had to collect bark from the tree and carefully place it in a basket. The fairies and baby fairies would be asleep in the bark. I *knew* I'd take most of them, but not all of them. I also *knew*, somehow, that I was to bring silver coins, honey, and a shiny gift to leave at the base of the tree. I had to carry a small bell with me and, most importantly, *I had to do it two days from then.* I could feel an urgency again. Time was growing short.

"I still didn't know WHY I had to do this, but I was delighted that information was bubbling up with a strange certainty that made me put all doubts out of my mind. I wrote it all down in my journal so I wouldn't forget anything. I committed to following through.

"It would be Saturday in two days, and that was perfect because my son, your dad, would be with his grandparents, and I would have time to carry out this plan."

Alma reached over and touched my arm when she referenced my dad. I put my hand on top of hers and leaned in. Alma looked straight into my eyes as she described what happened next.

"Then it occurred to me, *What would I do with the fairies once I collected them? Where would I take them?* Almost instantaneously, just as I thought the questions, the answer came to mind."

Alma rocked back in her chair and hit the heel of her hand on her forehead, as if she just had a bright idea. "I knew *exactly where* I was supposed to take them! How had I not thought of it sooner?"

I felt the excitement myself, so I stood up, jumped up and down and chimed in. "Oh good, Grandma! Did you decide to take them back to the woods behind your little red house?"

Alma grinned big. "Oh, wow, Kaiah, I didn't think of that back then. That's a great idea, but no, that wasn't the place. But, there *was* a place, a 140-acre stretch of woods, fields, and open sky just about twenty minutes from where I lived. It was private land owned by my friend, Alice. It was a safe place, and I knew it was the right place."

I could feel myself smiling as Alma spoke in anticipation of her whole plan coming together.

She went on. "It was before the days we carried cellphones with us everywhere. I had to run home and was excited to call Alice and tell her my realization. I was going to ask her if I could bring fairies to live in her woods. But Alice didn't know anything about the fairies yet. As soon as she answered the phone, my excitement ebbed and I felt a rush of heat and hesitation rise up in my cheeks.

"On the other end of the phone I heard Alice inquire, 'Are you okay? Tell me. What's going on?'

"Suddenly, I wasn't sure I should tell her. How could I? I didn't have any idea how she'd respond."

Alma held her hand up to her ear as if it was a phone and altered her voice to sound like Alice talking. "'Is everything okay? I can tell something is going on. Just spit it out.' Alice said."

Alma talked in her regular voice again. "Alice's voice was kind and reassuring. Soon, my commitment to see this through overrode my uncertainty and my story tumbled out.

"Alice listened quietly on the other end of the phone as I told her about that morning on March 13th. I wished I could see the expression on her face. Was she listening? Smiling? Did she think I was crazy?"

Alma looked at me in a crazy way again, rolling her eyes and sticking out her tongue. I laughed, but as I listened, I felt a sense of magic building, as if we were right on the edge of something extraordinary.

She continued, "Finally, I said, 'Alice, the real reason I'm calling is...' But before I could finish, Alice cut me off. Without a hint of skepticism, she said, 'Yes! Yes! You want to bring the fairies here, right? That's why your're calling, isn't it? Yes, yes! You're welcome to bring them here!'"

Alma slouched back in her chair, looking utterly spent, and let out a long sigh.

"Kaiah," she said, "in that moment, my fear dissolved, and I was so relieved. It was a gift that day to share my story and to have Alice completely embrace it.

"Later, Alice told me she'd felt a fluttering in her stomach when I called, even before I told her my story. She told me that when I started talking about the fairies, she just *knew* I'd be bringing them to her land. It was as if she knew before I even asked her. Like it was all pre-arranged.

"It was amazing the many ways things appeared to be effortlessly falling into place. It was more than just synchronicity. I was being guided. Although, remembering all of this now, in retrospect, I shouldn't have been surprised."

Alma smiled softly and added, "I hung up the phone feeling like something was guiding me. Maybe the fairies had arranged it all. Maybe it was chance or fate. Whatever it was, I felt more confident. It was coming together. I wasn't alone, and now I finally had a plan."

II

MOVING DAY ARRIVES

"I got up early Saturday morning, prepared to devote the day to believing in something I couldn't see nor explain in a rational way. I felt good though, energized and vibrantly alive.

"As day began to break, I could see it was overcast with a murky, gray sky, and a misty rain was falling. There were no signs of the weather changing anytime soon."

Alma pointed up to the sky which we could see from our seats on the porch. I kept my eyes on her hand and then expanded my gaze into the clouds above as she stated the obvious.

"That day was very similar to the weather we have here today. No sun. Everything dreary and damp, " Alma said, raising her voice as she pointed up to the sky.

She continued, "Jason called that morning and asked if I wanted him to come along. At first, I said no, but then, a voice inside my head said, '*He has to come.*' It wasn't just a passing thought; it was a deep, gut-sort-of-knowing. A premonition?

Intuition? Instruction from the fairies? I didn't know. What I did know was that I needed to listen to it. I was trying to grasp the whole idea when Jason's voice broke in to confirm what I already knew.

"He said with certainty, 'Hey, I think I am *supposed* to go with you. I had a dream last night and in that dream I went along.'

"There was silence between us. I was trying to grasp what was happening when I heard his voice on the other end of the phone, 'Hello, hello, are you there?'

"I answered, 'Yes, I'm here. So, you had a dream, did you?'

"It was obvious to me, Kaiah, that neither of us were in control of this adventure. After a pause, without further discussion, I said I'd welcome his company and told Jason to get to my house as fast as he could."

I stopped Alma for a minute to tell her how much I loved this part. I loved that Jason had a dream and that both of them followed it. Alma had taught me that dreams are important. If I was moving fairies, I think I would want someone with me. I wanted to know what happened next.

"Well," Alma said as she rubbed her hands together, "it was such a rush that morning. Looking back, I can't imagine it any other way. Jason arrived quickly and the morning was still young.

"Rain continued to fall upon a silent earth. Jason offered to drive and I accepted. When we got to the woods, he parked, turned off the motor, and silently looked at me. I told him I needed to do this part alone. He nodded in agreement without saying a word, as if he expected it to be no different.

"I got out of the car alone and walked to the line of trees at the edge of the road. I asked the land if I could enter, but I didn't hear or feel anything. I took a step. I didn't see or sense anything. Everything was quiet.

"I wanted to turn around and get back in the car and have Jason take me out for breakfast. I looked back at the waiting vehicle. He smiled at me with a casual grin and motioned with his hand to go on. Seeing him there, calm and steady, with no sign of doubt, gave me the courage to turn around and face the woods again."

Alma was picking her feet up and slowly placing them back on the floor to demonstrate the pace of her steps.

"I took another tentative step. The green underbrush along the roadside was spotted with ferns, may apples, and ragweed. Patches of St. John's Wort and purple asters stood looking forlorn in the drizzle.

"Then I noticed something. Right in front of me was a circular patch of brilliant light shining onto the ground. It reminded me of a floodlight shining down onto a stage. I looked up yet saw no source for the light. The sky was a solid blanket of hazy cloud cover. I looked down and the light remained.

"I stepped toward the light. It moved a step ahead of me, as if leading the way. I followed it. By now, I was somewhat familiar with the physical sensations I felt whenever the fairies were near, even if I couldn't see them: a subtle dizziness, a strong sense of being in the moment, a sharp alertness. The world felt calm and quiet. I had a feeling I was not alone. I tried to focus on what I'd come to do."

As Alma took a deep breath and a pause, I sheepishly said, "I love that. I love how the fairies made a light for you."

"Yes, Kaiah, it was special. The light led me right to the tree where I'd seen the fairies and disappeared into it. I noticed the tree looked different now. It had a strange appearance, with all of the bark curled away from the trunk in strips, as if someone had partially peeled it back."

Alma had a small tablet on the table, and she quickly drew a sketch of a tree with the bark rolled back. I wondered how a tree could do such a thing. If the fairies did it, then how?

She continued as we looked at the drawing. "I wondered how I would get the bark off the tree. I'd packed a knife, even though the fairies never mentioned bringing one. I guess they knew I wouldn't need it. The bark was already loose. All I had to do was take it.

"Standing there, looking at that tree, I felt the urge to cry. There was something so humbling about that moment. I was in the presence of something I couldn't explain, and yet it all felt so sacred, precious, and loving. I felt more alive than I'd ever felt in my life. I realized how delicate life really is."

Alma stopped talking then. Looking back, I don't think I fully understood why my grandmother seemed sad. It seemed like an exciting adventure to me. Still, something in me understood it was best to remain silent at that moment. Alma had taught me about the power of silence and simply sitting together. She sat quietly for several minutes. I didn't want to disturb her, so I just waited, drawing pictures of trees on the tablet until she was ready to begin again.

"You know, Kaiah, it's hard to tell this story because so much of it exists beyond words or clear explanation. I simply *knew* things without understanding why or how I knew them. Each time I needed to know something it arrived, as long as I patiently stayed open and receptive.

"It was hard to surrender, though... exciting and scary at the same time. Adults today aren't always good at this sort of thing. I think we forget how to do it. Don't you ever forget, Kaiah. Never forget."

Alma emphasized my name and reached over and squeezed my hand. Now, as an adult myself, I know grown-ups can complicate matters as we try to make five-year plans, rush around with our busy lives, and try to intellectualize and rationalize every decision and goal. We have a hard time being in the moment, listening to that quiet voice within, and slowing down to notice the subtle worlds of energy around us. Surrendering to the unknown is rare. Still, I try to remember her words.

Alma began reviewing the directions she was given.

"I *knew* I needed to collect the bark and the fairies would be in it. I knew the two fairies I met in the woods would be staying behind because they told me so, ~ '*We will stay behind with some others, but the rest of them, along with the babies, will go with you.*'

"The wordless instructions I had been given just days earlier echoed in my mind now. I *knew* I needed to burn sage to create smoke when the babies were asleep, ~ '*They will have been put to sleep to avoid unnecessary trauma during the move. Handle them with care. Burn some sage when you arrive. The smoke will ease the transition, calm you, and lull them into a deeper sleep as they move from our world into yours, if only for a while.*'

"I *knew* I had to ring the bell three times before I left the tree, a simple but necessary gesture to mark the transition, ~ '*Ring the bell three times once you have collected all the bark,*' they had said, '*And ring it three times again when you have placed them in their new home to awaken them.*' Each detail fell into place with this quiet instruction given exactly in order of need.

"Before collecting the bark, I put out the honey, coins, and a few shiny things I had brought from home. I started to peel strips of bark off the tree and put them in the basket. I kept doing it until I was told, *'Good, you have them all.'*

"I rang the bell as instructed. Then I said goodbye with a full heart and a silent prayer for the safety of those left behind. I headed back to the car carrying the basket and the weight of responsibility.

"As I got in the car, Jason smiled as if all of this was perfectly normal, and asked, 'You got 'em?'

"I nodded.

"He said, 'Okay, let's go to Alice's then.'

"'Yep, let's go' was all I could say as I held the basket tight in my lap."

12

JOURNEY TO THE DESTINATION

Alma looked at me directly then and asked if I was okay. She must have seen the intense look on my face. I was worried about what was going to happen to the fairies.

Alma said, "What's the matter? Are you comfortable? Do you need anything?"

"I'm fine," I answered. "I guess I'm just worried about the fairies."

Alma told me she was worried at the time, too, and her expression told me she understood my feelings. She was biting her lower lip and recomposed herself.

Then she began again. "When we arrived at Alice's place, I was somewhat surprised that no one was home. After a moment, though, I realized it probably was for the best. I didn't want distractions.

"We drove up the hill on the property to a place where there was a large stone circle ~ a medicine wheel ~ constructed on the earth. Alice and I and some other friends built it years before. We buried crystals, herbs, and prayers in the earth and had large stone boulders placed on the perimeter. There was a large tree stump in the center. The circle was used for times of gatherings, seasonal celebrations, and healing rituals. I felt right at home.

"I got out of the car with the basket and headed to the stump. Without any discussion, Jason got out of the car and came with me this time. There were large expanses of open fields and a pond in front of us. Behind us stretched over a hundred acres of pristine forested land.

"Jason asked, in a curious tone, 'Now what?'

"I looked at him bewildered because I suddenly realized I had NO IDEA what to do next! It hadn't occurred to me to ask WHAT TO DO once I got there, and I let Jason know. The only thing they *told* me was that I needed *to ring the bell to awaken them* after we put them in their new home. But where was their new home? We had 140 acres to choose from!"

I laughed at Alma. "That is so funny," I said, "You must have found a place, though, right? I mean, what did you do?"

"Well, it is funny, I suppose, in retrospect," Alma said. "First of all, Jason told me not to panic. We began to discuss options. We considered just leaving them there in the medicine wheel, but I had a vague feeling we were rushing matters. The large stone circle was too exposed and it didn't feel right.

"I sat down on one of the stones, kicked off my shoes, closed my eyes, and took a few deep breaths like I had done with the woman at the festival. I tried to relax my whole body. I knew I needed to sit and calmly think this through. Maybe an insight would come. I stayed like that for about ten minutes until my mind felt calmer. Jason waited patiently and quietly.

"Not sure what else to do, I silently prayed to every guiding and divine power in the universe that I could think of for help: Dear *God, fairy folk, guardians, angels, spirit guides, Jesus, ancestors, Great Mystery, Great Goddess, Divine Universe, Mother Earth, Mother Mary, spirits of the land, HELP ME! Please! What do we do now?*"

I couldn't help but laugh at Alma's prayer. I could imagine her calling upon every helping source she could think of in her time of need. We do that, don't we? In our times of need. Even as a child, I saw the humor in it and the reason for it.

Alma winked at me, let out a chuckle, and said, "I had to call in the troops! Right? Sometimes we do need lots of help!"

We both laughed while she fussed with some crumbs on the table.

"Sitting in that stone circle, my bare feet pressed to the wet earth, the quiet of the forest behind me, made the moment feel timeless," she said. "I felt connected to humans of all times who had touched the earth and her mysteries and who may have called out into the silence for help. As I waited, I could feel a warm tingling in my ears, especially my left, and a slight pressure on my forehead. My solar plexus, here in center of my body, felt like it was spinning. I kept trying to breathe and relax.

"After a few minutes, I started to notice movement in my visual field and something floating across my inner vision off in the distance. It was out of focus at first, but I could tell it was moving slowly toward me. Something was emerging from a misty landscape. Then suddenly, the image sharpened in my mind, and I saw a monk, a holy man, standing before me!"

My mouth was half open at the idea of my grandma seeing a monk. I imagined a solemn figure in a brown robe standing in front of her. Alma must have noticed my reaction.

She paused, cleared her throat, and said, "You know how it works, Kaiah. We close our eyes and see with our imaginations. That's how the monk visited me, through my inner sight. You know our imagination is more than just a place of pretend. It's a gateway, a portal into the soul realms, the spirit realms, and the creative realms if we learn how to access them."

I nodded, knowing exactly what she meant. It was one of my favorite things to do with her. Alma was an artist too, and when we painted together she had me use my imagination to create works of art.

She also had me imagine beautiful, peaceful places in my mind when I was worried or anxious, and it helped me to relax. Sometimes we talked to animals that way, and sometimes we used our inner sight to send loving prayers to others.

Alma closed her eyes as if she was journeying right then. She confirmed what I was imagining when she said, "The man looked like an old-time monk in a brown robe."

Alma began moving her arms and continued, "He was jumping around waving his arms frantically as if to get my attention. He made me laugh a little. Jason interrupted then and asked me what was happening and why I was laughing.

"Without moving or opening my eyes, I said to him, 'Wait a minute. Give me another minute. I think I am getting something here.'

"Jason, God bless him, knew enough to be quiet and wait. I turned my attention back to the monk.

"In my mind's eye, I playfully asked, *So, what do you want? Am I to assume I have a Christian monk assisting with fairy relocation?*

"The man crossed his arms and looked at me as if he didn't appreciate my humor and said with a rather impatient tone, *Yes, as a matter of fact, I have information for you. If you'd like to hear it. Unless I'm not the right messenger for you.*

"I smiled at his response, *Okay, okay. I didn't mean to offend you. I did ask for help, and you came. So, yes, I do want your help. I believe I am supposed to leave these fairies here in the forest and awaken them, but I don't know what to do with them now that we're here. Can I leave them here in the stone circle?*

"*No, no!* he said curtly and then proceeded to give me very specific directions.

"He said, *Turn around and walk back to the road. Turn right and head toward the house. Then take the first path on your left into the forest. Walk 45 steps, then turn left. Walk 15 more steps and stop. You'll know what to do from there.*

"I looked at him a bit skeptically, but before I could say anything, he said, as if reading my thoughts before I formed them, *Since you don't seem to have any ideas of your own, you might as well try following mine.*

"Then he crossed his arms in exasperation, rolled his eyes, and impatiently looked away.

"I was quickly becoming fond of this snarky monk, and he had a point. So, after repeating his directions to make sure I got them correct, I thanked him and bid him farewell. He waved goodbye over his shoulder as he hastily disappeared back into the mist.

"I opened my eyes. The air felt electric and alive. I turned to Jason who was staring intently at me as if he was about to burst.

"I said, 'Hey, okay, this is what I got. So, this monk just told me...'

"Jason, who looked thoroughly soaked standing there in the rain, interrupted me again before I could finish.

"'Wait! Wait!' he raised his hands, palms facing me, as if to stop me from speaking. 'This who? A monk? You saw a monk?'

"He kept repeating it. 'A monk? A monk knows what to do with fairies?'

"He started muttering, half talking to himself, 'Well, we *are* carrying fairies around in a picnic basket, so I guess listening to a monk in your imagination giving us directions isn't the strangest thing we've done today!'

"He threw his arms up over his head and spun around in exasperation. He faced me again, not really knowing what to do with himself, and stood in silence with his arms crossed.

"'Okay,' he said, 'tell me.'

"I giggled, wiped the rain away from my eyes, and paused to thank him for coming along with me. I told him I could hardly believe it myself, but I did see a monk, and he gave me very clear directions. Since we didn't have another plan, I thought we should give it a try. I told him exactly what the monk had said to me.

"Jason agreed. There was nothing else to go on. We decided to trust the directions we were given and started down the road. We turned onto the first path to our left."

13

IN MEASURED STEPS

I was captivated by Alma's story, imagining it right along with her. Still, it was hard for my ten-year-old body to sit still as I listened. I stood up and leaned against the table and then stretched back against the porch railing. Alma didn't seem bothered by my moving around. I could tell she was enjoying her memories.

She said, "We counted our steps in the rain-soaked forest, each footfall sinking into the soft earth. 'One, two, three... forty-three, forty-four, forty-five.'

"When we finally turned left off the path, the under-growth thickened, and I couldn't help but wonder if we truly were heading in the right direction. We started counting to fifteen with each step, 'One, two, three...'

"Jason whispered, 'This is insane.' I sort of agreed with him. But at this point, there was no turning back.

"... thirteen, fourteen, fifteen. We stopped and found ourselves standing right in the middle of a perfect circle of moss in an otherwise unruly forest floor.

"Jason looked at me with a smile and shook his head. I didn't know what he was smiling about and said so.

"He began to explain, 'Do you know what this is? Do you know what we're standing in?'

"I looked around for a clue and then said, 'No. What is it?'

"'This is a fairy circle,' he exclaimed, turning around in the space. 'You know, a circle of moss where fairies play!'

"I looked at him with amazement. 'What? Really? How do you know that? Are you serious?'

"He confidently said, 'Yes, I was just reading about fairy circles the other day. I started looking up fairy lore after you told me your story.'"

I stopped my grandma then, unable to contain my own curiosity.

"A fairy circle?" I repeated. "That is so amazing. In the middle of the woods? Have we ever seen fairy circles before?"

"It's possible," she said.

I clapped my hands with excitement, feeling the air around us hum with something ancient and magical. Even though I wasn't sure if 'd ever seen a fairy circle, I easily could imagine it.

I urged her to continue. She began again. "So, I just stood there with rain dripping off the ends of my hair, mouth hanging open, not knowing what to make of it all. I turned to Jason, placed the basket of bark down in the moss, and continued to ponder this mystery.

"I said, 'A fairy circle? Hmm... I guess I shouldn't be surprised. So do we leave them here? In the fairy circle? Does this feel right?'

"Jason shook his head. 'Well, ... I don't know.'

"His voice was laced with frustration and urgency. 'Why don't you ask the monk?'

"I shot him a glance, raising an eyebrow, and reminded him what the monk told me ~ *You will know what to do once you get there.* Jason looked at me and sort of huffed. He seemed restless.

"I closed my eyes to see if I actually could get the monk to talk to me again. Nothing happened. Then, with my eyes still closed, a thought entered my mind. It felt like fairy communication again. The words formed on their own.

"'*From here, Jason knows the way!*'

"My eyes snapped open, and before I could say anything, I saw Jason standing at the edge of the circle, his back to me, his gaze fixed deeper into the woods.

"My body tingled with a sensation of pins and needles all over. There was a sense of something moving around us. I felt like the land was shifting.

"Jason turned to me with wild eyes and a big grin, and half hollered, 'I know where to take them from here! It's that big ol' beech tree. Come on, I'll show you!'

"He took off, almost running. I quickly picked up the basket to follow him.

"Water was dripping everywhere."

14

MOTHER OF THE FOREST

"When we reached the tree, I saw it was indeed a huge old beech, truly a grandmother of trees."

Alma leaned forward and said, "Kaiah, you know, beech trees are the ones with elephant-like legs, deep gray, solid, and wrapped in smooth bark."

I knew she had spoken to me about them in the past. My grandma's fondness for trees was apparent. Alma paused to pour us more juice and placed a warm oat and berry muffin in front of each of us. I absent-mindedly picked up my muffin and took a bite. Alma, diverting from her story for a few moments, began to muse all about beech trees.

She explained that in the botanical genus *Fagus*, there are about a dozen recognized species native to the Northern Hemisphere. True beech trees, left undisturbed, can live to be three hundred years old. Some live even longer.

Alma told me the beech tree offers shelter and sustenance to many creatures of the forest. The bark, leaves, and nuts offer a variety of medicinal remedies and provide wood for various human endeavors.

She was sure to inform me that beech trees were in danger from diseases, climate change, and other human impacts. She said that we may not be able to fix all the problems, but it's important to educate ourselves and to be mindful of them in our prayers.

Alma also added some folklore. "There was so much I didn't understand back then, but I've since learned that in British folklore, the beech tree is called 'Queen of the Trees,' 'Mother of the Forest,' and the oak is the King."

My grandma sat up straight, proud of her discovery and amused by it all. She slapped her knee and added, "Do you get it? The fairies had led us right to the Queen, a perfect place for relocating fairy babies, wouldn't you say?"

Alma's enthusiasm was palpable. I giggled as I imagined little fairies settling into their new home in the Mother of the Forest.

After a deep breath, and without further delay, she picked up where she left off. "At that point, after we arrived at the beech tree, Jason and I silently stood looking at it as if we had found a sacred and ancient site. The dull light of the low gray sky and drizzling rain softened the entire scene. A light fog had descended and all was still.

"I finally broke the silence and asked, 'Do we leave them here around the base of the tree?'

"Jason looked perplexed. Then, in his matter-of-fact tone, he said, 'I don't know. Let me ask the tree.'

"He said this so seriously and sincerely, as if it was the most normal and natural thing in the world to say ~ *Let me ask the tree.* It sounded completely rational to me in that moment. I just had to trust that Jason would be able to talk to *this* tree.

"He put his hands on the trunk and closed his eyes. I waited. And waited. I was very glad Jason had come with me.

"After a little time passed, he turned to me with an excited expression. His eyes were sparkling again. I felt my heart up in my throat.

"'No. No,' he said, '*not around* the base of the tree. The tree said we need to put them IN *the tree.*'

"I blinked hard. I heard what he said, but my mind was scrambling to comprehend what I heard. I could feel my brain forming a question. Only a few seconds passed before our eyes met and his expression matched my own.

How in the world could we put them IN the tree?"

15

HOME SWEET HOME

"We stood there, soaking wet, staring at the tree, dumbfounded. I still held the basket in my hands.

"At the same time, something told me Jason was right. Without saying a word, he reached over and touched the tree once more. His eyes closed again as he listened intently.

"The odd sensation of time standing still hovered nearby. It felt spacious and present. My senses were heightened. I thought these were signs we were getting closer. I hoped an answer would come... and it did.

"Finally, Jason turned to me and said, 'You have to get on my shoulders.'

"'Whaat?' I blurted out.

"Unable to hide my amusement, I burst into laughter at the whole scene. There was something so playful and joyful bubbling just underneath all the seriousness. He laughed, too. The laughter was deep and tender. We were getting giddy.

"I wiped the rain from my eyes again and while still smiling, asked, 'And why would I need to get on your shoulders?'

"He paused for a moment, clearly unsure of how to explain, then replied, 'I don't know how all of this is working. I just know you need to get on my shoulders. Okay? Trust me. And... actually... I think this is why I had to come with you.'

"That gave me pause and I realized what he said was true."

I couldn't help but giggle as Alma described the scene. I thought it was funny imagining them in the rain, trying to figure it all out. I said so to Alma and added, "It's a good thing he went along with you, wasn't it? So, did you get on his shoulders?"

Alma responded with a chuckle, "Oh dear girl, it is a bit funny, isn't it? It was good he came along. I'm glad you're enjoying the story. That's why I wanted to share it with you. It really is a delight to recall it."

I settled back into the big, soft rose-colored cushions, pulled up my pink sweater, and folded my hands to show I was ready for her to go on with the story. I asked, "So, did you get on his shoulders?"

Alma continued, "Jason was about six feet tall, and I was five feet and four inches. Together, when I stood on his shoulders, we were about eleven feet tall.

"He looked up at the tree, his face serious, and said, 'The tree told me there's an opening up higher. Look for it.'

"This was important information. We looked all around the tree, but we couldn't see any opening from the ground. As improbable as it was, Jason silently looked at me with eyes of certainty. I simply shook my head, handed him the basket, kicked off my shoes, and climbed onto his shoulders.

"Slowly, we circled around the tree. I was hugging the tree as we inched our way around the trunk. Smooth, solid bark remained inches from my face as I tried to keep myself steady.

Then, my outstretched hand felt something bumpy. As I got closer, I realized it was a large, circular opening in the trunk. Inside was a large open space lined with moss that seemed to extend inward over half the circumference of the trunk itself.

"The opening was level with my face. It hadn't been visible from the ground, and it was protected from the weather by overhanging bark. I felt tears well up out of the sheer perfection of the moment. I was motionless and speechless until Jason reminded me I was standing on his shoulders. He asked what I saw.

"My stomach churned with emotion. I quietly said, 'There is an opening in the tree. It's beautiful. It's perfect. This is like a miracle. I can't believe it.'

"Jason, still holding me up from below, said, 'Well, that is amazing for sure, but hurry up and believe it. Here, take the basket. Let's hurry this miracle along!' His patience and practicality were charming."

Alma smiled warmly at that memory. I was imagining her standing on Jason's shoulders. I could see the whole thing unfold in my imagination.

She began again. "I took the basket and slowly placed all the pieces of bark, with the fairies and their babies, into the hole. The moss inside the tree was a velvety green pillow that sparkled even in the dim light. Once I finished, I handed the basket back to Jason and pulled the bell from my pocket. I rang it once.

"I was worried I was doing it all wrong. I wasn't sure what would happen or how to know if I was doing it right. Then I rang the bell a second time. Instantly, a bright ray of light burst into the hole. It was so sudden and unexpected, it startled me."

Alma stopped speaking again. Her gaze wandered off into the distance and her hands were raised as if she was touching the tree. While I waited for her to continue, I imagined the light shining in the hole as it illuminated the glistening moss. I partially leaned onto her lap and put my head on her chest. Alma pulled me close. She kept hold of me as she continued, using only one hand to manifest her memory.

"The light continued to illuminate the entire cavity in the tree. I couldn't see the sun in the sky and had no idea where it was coming from. It literally took my breath away. I felt as if I was in the presence of something very holy and precious. I remember thinking, *we found home in more ways than one.*

"Then with tears in my eyes and my voice trembling, I said to Jason, 'Oh my goodness, the light, it's shining in here. It's so... beautiful.'"

Alma hugged me even tighter.

"I rang the bell a third time as instructed," she said, "and tears finally flowed down my face from all the emotions racing through me. It was done. My heart burst open with joy and love. I knew I had done the right thing. I never saw a fairy that day, but I trusted they were safe now.

"Jason helped me down. We stood a little while longer at the base of the tree. In silence, we walked back to the car.

"Exhausted, but giddy, we spent the ride home retelling every detail of the day."

16

CONFIRMATIONS COME

"**A**fter that day, life returned to normal. I still wondered about the fairies from time to time. *Were they real? Had I imagined it all?* Then I remembered how things happened and how guided I felt. I knew it was far more than make-believe. I remembered the light and the joy. I couldn't question it.

"I was glad for the choice I had made, but being human, I complicated matters by wishing I had *proof* or a clear explanation. That was not meant to be. I think there are some mysteries beyond our human understanding, as smart as we think we are.

"I did my best to accept the experience for what it was, or what I thought it was, and went on with my life. But..." Alma lowered her chin, peering at me over the rim of her glasses for emphasis. "... in time, I would learn the fairies were not finished with me yet."

I squealed, "Yippee! You mean the story isn't over?"

Alma shook her head, "No, it isn't."

Then I asked, "Grandma, if so many people around the world say they see fairies, why don't more people believe in them?"

Alma responded kindly, "Yes, dear, that is a very good question. I'm happy to hear you asking questions. When it comes to things mysterious and unknown, asking good questions is a wonderful skill to develop.

"In truth, I'm afraid there isn't a good or clear answer to your question. I think humanity has a tendency to fear or deny what it can't understand or perceive with the five senses. There are a lot of stories about encounters with otherworldly beings identified as fairies, but our world is good at doubting such things. It is good to be skeptical, of course, but it's also wise to stay open to wonder and possibilities. At least, its more fun that way."

That satisfied me for the moment, although over the years, we have had more conversations about many kinds of mysteries and *what they all mean.* Such conversations are treasured times with my grandma.

Alma returned to her story, "A couple of weeks after we relocated the fairies, I was driving home on Belleview Road. That drive took me past the woods where I first had seen the lights. I wasn't prepared for what I was about to witness.

"As I rounded the bend, I had an odd sense of vertigo. Something was wrong. My mind was trying to make sense of the scene before me. My whole body stiffened and I felt sick to my stomach. I pulled the car over and stopped.

"Forcing myself out of my car, I stood still with a rising sense of grief. The forest was gone. It was clear-cut. Gone."

I gasped out loud when Alma said this. I covered my mouth with my hands while she continued to describe the incident.

"I slowly walked to the clearing and stumbled over broken branches and severed limbs to the single tree that remained. Surprisingly, or perhaps not so surprisingly, the only tree that still stood was the one from which the fairies had emerged. The rest of the wooded area was cut back to the creek. It appeared a new house was going to be built.

"Here it was. The explanation...*the sense of urgency.* This is why I had to move the fairies. They must have known this was going to happen!! The forest was gone. It was a sad confirmation."

Alma grew silent. I wanted to say something, yet no words came. I just watched my grandmother's face, the soft blinking of her eyes, her chest moving with each breath. The weight of the moment settled in.

As I reflect back, it occurs to me that Alma's experience as a child in the Adirondacks foreshadowed what she would experience later with the fairies. I also realize now that her experiences were not just about those woods and those fairies. It was about the human condition and our relationship, or lack thereof, with the earth. It was about witnessing the loss of so many wild places and the inhabitants of those wild places, both seen and unseen. It was about human disregard, or perhaps our thoughtlessness to even consider how our actions might impact the world around us. We seldom say please or thank you to the natural world for what we take and use. I realize, like my grandmother does, that humans have a right to thrive and use resources, too. How we use them and how we relate to them become bigger questions.

A bit uncomfortable with the intensity of the moment and not knowing what else to say, I whispered, "Grandma, why do people cut down trees?"

Alma took my hand. "Well, dear, we do live here on the planet too. Humans use wood for many things and its not all bad. We use it to build homes and make paper. We use it for heat and to make furniture. The resources are ours to use for our survival, but often wc take too much or sometimes we take without thinking much about the impact it has on others. We often fail to find alternatives and fail to live in harmony. It is a good question to ask, and it is a very complicated answer."

I nodded respectfully at her answer. Seamlessly, she resumed her story.

"I touched the tree and thought, or hoped, I could feel the fairies who had stayed behind. Were they watching? Witnessing?

"Then again, like shifting sands, an inner spaciousness arose and telepathically I heard these words: 'It *will be okay. Balance always is restored. With change and destruction comes new birth, new beginnings. Do not be sad for us. Thank you for helping.*' And that was the last time the fairies of Belleview Road ever spoke to me.

"In spite of their comforting message, I headed for home feeling overwhelmed, confused, and heartbroken."

Alma sat back in her chair and made an audible exhalation. I was feeling emotional myself. She patted the hand I had placed on her knee to comfort her. I waited in silence.

After a few minutes, she smiled, gave me a hug around my shoulders, and said, "Oh, but still the fairies were not done with me. Truly, as I think back now, I'm amazed at how perfectly timed everything was. It was heartbreaking and yet absolutely beautiful at the same time. All of it. I never could've imagined it. But the story is not over yet."

I was delighted to hear her say that and told her so.

I said, "Oh, I'm so glad it isn't over yet! But wait! You said you never talked to the fairies again."

"Well yes, that's true," Alma said. "That day was the last time they spoke to me, but not the last time I was aware of them. There's a little more to the story."

"Oh good, go on," I urged.

Alma kept trying to brush away a bee hovering around our table, then continued in a serious tone.

"After seeing the spectacle of the clear-cut, I went straight home. As I was unlocking my front door, the phone was ringing. Answering the phone, I discovered Alice at the other end. Her voice was full of excitement. I couldn't have guessed, in a million years, what she was about to tell me!

"As I listened on the phone, Alice's voice was high and she started off slowly enunciating her words. 'Oh, have I... GOT... A STORY... TO TELL... YOU!' Then she started speaking faster, 'I know you're supposed to know about this! I had to call you right away! This is your confirmation!! If you doubted if the fairies are real, you won't doubt it now!'

"I really had no idea what she was talking about and she asked me if I was sitting down, which I was not, so I pulled up a chair and took a seat. Now I really was getting curious.

"Alice was about to tell me something that countered the devastation I had just seen. Looking back now, I think the fairies were giving something back to me for helping them. They were opening my heart to a world more vast, interconnected, and indescribable than I could've imagined on my own. And in sharing my story, others now were reflecting its truth back to me. It was a shared adventure. I was about to see the seeds of new beginnings."

Once again, in my youthful impatience, I had to interrupt my grandmother who was trailing off in her own thoughts again.

"Alma! Come on! I can't wait. Tell me! What did Alice tell you?!"

"Alright, alright, yes, let's get to it," Alma said as she rolled her eyes at me.

"Well, after that, Alice continued in her excited voice explaining that her family had gathered at her home for a picnic that day. Remember, she lived in a house located on the 140 acres where I rehoused the fairies. There were small children at the gathering and, after lunch, the children said they were going to go play in the woods. So, off they went.

"Alice told me that after a few hours the children came running back. They were excited and wanted the adults to come see what they'd made in the woods. The adults, grumbling a little, finally gathered themselves and headed up the path to find out what all the excitement was about. The children ran ahead of them.

"'You're not going to believe this,' Alice said. 'Well, yes, YOU will...' she teased. She also wanted to be sure I understood that she had *not* uttered one word to anyone about the fairies, the tree, or what I had done.

"As they kept walking, Alice started to get a tingling in her body and realized they were headed straight for that large beech tree. The children surrounded the tree yelling, 'Look, *what we made! Look what we made! We made houses for the fairies!'"*

I think I startled Alma as I jumped to my feet at the thought of the children making fairy houses! I clapped my hands, jumping up and down, and spun around in a circle.

Alma laughed and clapped with me.

"It WAS exciting," Alma affirmed.

"Alice told me she was amazed that out of 140 acres of woodland, the children picked *that* tree to surround with fairy houses! Alice admitted she had no idea how such at thing was possible and wished I'd been there."

With a deep breath, Alma paused and then added, "The fairies had houses and I sat on the other end of the phone speechless. I had no rational explanation either. I told Alice I didn't need to be there because I knew what she said was true."

I leaned against my Alma, rested my head on her shoulder. Again, she made room for me to squeeze in beside her. Even now, all these years later, I remember what that felt like. The joy, the laughter, the intimacy, the smell of her, the softness of her body, the warmth of her embrace, the feeling of being safe and believing all was right with the world in that moment.

17

COMING FULL CIRCLE

Alma said she needed to stretch her legs for a minute and get some more hot water for her tea. She asked if I wanted anything but I was content. I sat quietly on the porch as she went into the house.

The day remained dreary and I saw a couple of squirrels running between trees in the distance. It was so peaceful, though. I picked up the tablet from the table and started drawing on it again. I tried drawing what I thought a fairy might look like. Soon, Alma was back with her hot tea and settled into her chair. I thought the story had probably come to an end with the fairy houses and said so.

"Was that the end of your story, Alma? That was a great story. Thank you for telling it to me."

She took a sip of her tea and slowly, methodically placed it in the saucer.

Then she said, "Well, Kaiah, sometimes it's hard to tell where a story really begins or when it ends. As far as this story goes, all I can say is I didn't hear anything about fairies again until fifteen years later.

I perked up. "Wow, wait, there's more?" I put my elbows on the table and leaned on it.

Alma nodded. "Yep. Fifteen years passed. Life had moved on."

"Fifteen years?" I repeated to clarify. "Did you see the fairies again?"

"Oh, no dear. I never saw the fairies again. But one day, I heard a knock on my door."

Alma knocked three times on the arm of the chair and paused. I could tell she was being dramatic.

"When I opened the door, I saw a woman standing on my porch. I knew her as an acquaintance. She looked nervous and near to tears. I wasn't sure if she was okay.

"I said, 'Hello, may I help you?'

"Biting her lip and looking as though she might turn and run, she said, 'I know this sounds crazy, but I think I need your help. I don't know why exactly, but I was told to come talk to you... that you could help me. Alice... Alice told me to find you.'

"I could not imagine what this was about. She seemed so nervous. I asked her to come in. Once inside, she seemed to calm down a bit and took a few deep breaths. I encouraged her to tell me how I could help her. Then her story spilled out.

"She began. 'You see, there is this place, this land, a couple of hours from town, and I think, well, I know this sounds crazy, but I think there are fairies there. It sounds even crazier now that I'm here saying it out loud to you. I'm afraid something bad is going to happen on this land. I have this strange feeling that I'm supposed to move the fairies. Does that sound crazy? I don't know what to do.'

"I sat there silently, trying to comprehend what the woman had said.

"She dropped her head and quietly added, 'I'm sorry... maybe this was a bad idea.'

"Finally, I found my words and said, 'Oh, no. No. You came to the right door. I don't think you're crazy. Alice was right to send you to me.

"I told her my own experience. I told her what the woman at the festival had told me. '*You have a choice. You can choose to believe it or not. You can choose to help them or not. What decision can you live with?*"

"She cried, as I had done, perhaps from the relief that someone understood. Then she hugged me for what seemed like a long time.

"She asked if I would come with her to the land and help. I admit, I really was tempted. However, I was leaving town later that very day to move to New Mexico for a job. I considered delaying my departure because a part of me really wanted to be near the fairies again, but something told me this was *her* journey, not mine. I declined, encouraged her, and wished her well.

"I never saw her again. I don't know what she decided to do. I believe that if she made her way to me that day, she probably has her own fairy story to tell.

"And I can rest in the knowing that when the fairies need our help, they find us. They find the ones who will listen. They find the ones who will risk believing."

Alma looked tired. She sat back and her shoulders relaxed. She looked across the yard as if searching for something and then said, "Kaiah, I think the most important thing to remember is that love matters. It matters in every realm. Humans often fear what they don't understand. It causes a lot of suffering. When we act with respect and compassion, even when we face the unknown, amazing things can happen."

I nodded in agreement. As I think back now, I know she wasn't just talking about fairies. She was talking about life and about how we treat each other and all living things. Embracing differences and acting lovingly toward what we might not understand is part of what makes humanity humane. It is a tall order but a hopeful one.

I could smell the lemon and ginger steeping in her tea as I asked her, "So, is that the end?"

"Yes, dear, for now, that is the end of my story." Alma sighed as she fanned herself with her napkin.

I didn't want it to end even though we had been at it for a while by then. It wasn't so much about the story anymore. I just didn't want the special time I was sharing with Alma to end. The next day would be her birthday, a cause for celebration, and we had housework to do. The whole family was coming.

I said, "Grandma, thank you for telling me about your fairies. I really liked your story."

She smiled tenderly and bowed her head.

"You are most welcome," she said, with a sense of humility.

Once again, the world was quiet around us.

A few minutes later, a bright light burst forth onto the ground right in front of the porch, even though the sky still appeared overcast. It was hard to miss. Thinking of Alma's story, I wondered if it was a sign from the fairies. Maybe they were pleased with the story, too.

Without warning, Alma jumped out of her chair, her arms raised to the sky.

And then, as if she was reading my mind, she said, "Look at that beautiful light shining there! It just might be a little nod from the fairies. Maybe they've been here listening to the story with us all along!"

She bent down close to my face, winked, poked me, and without waiting for me to respond, teased, "Hey, I'll race you for the last bowl of chocolate pudding!"

I think she let me get a head start as we both ran to the kitchen, laughing all the way.

EPILOGUE: KAIAH REFLECTS

As I reflect on that weekend, so much time has passed. However, I remember it as if it were yesterday. That weekend with Alma was so special.

I discovered her story didn't really end there. Stories never end, not really. It followed me, weaving its way into the quiet corners of my life, waiting to reveal more, to be shared again, and for me to evolve into my own part of the story.

I think about how Alma looked at me, the way her eyes twinkled when she said, "*They find the ones who listen.*" I imagine that is true for humans, too. We find each other through quiet cues and connections when the time is right. When we listen in the silence, we often are guided.

Sometimes, like right now, I just pause and take a few deep breaths.

Close my eyes.

Listen to the world.

Shift my awareness.

Life's creative, mystical, and divine energies move all around us and within us. They inform and inspire us and perhaps we help to inform and inspire them, too. It really is miraculous.

I am headed over to Alma's again soon. She still lives in the cottage by the creek and meadow. She is quieter now. Her time grows shorter in this world and still she wastes none of it. She is never without a tale to tell. She is a story-weaver. I can always find her there, by the fire, curled up with a blanket and some tea, where her heart resides and her stories linger.

Along the way, because of her stories, I have come to realize I have a choice in life. I can choose to believe in the inexplicable, or I can choose to disregard it. I can believe in the healing wisdom of nature, or I can ignore it. I can believe in the intricate interconnectedness of life, or I can deny it. I can choose to believe in the power of love in every realm, or I can doubt it.

Thanks to my grandma, my Alma, repeatedly, I've chosen to believe.

Above all, watch with glittering eyes the
whole world around you because the
greatest secrets are always hidden in the
most unlikely places.
~ Roald Dahl

PART III:

THIRTY YEARS LATER ...

The most beautiful and profound emotion we can express is the sensation of the mystical. It is the source of all true art and science. It is enough to know that what is impenetrable to us really exists, manifesting itself as the highest wisdom and the most radiant beauty, which our dull faculties can comprehend only in their primitive forms.
~ Albert Einstein (Living Philosophies, 1931)

STORY AS LIVING PRESENCE

*The world is full of magic things, patiently waiting
for our senses to grow sharper.*

~ W.B. Yeats

While my encounter with fairies was unique in my life, it was not the first time I'd encountered mystical or unusual things. When I was only six years old, for example, I had an experience in the woods behind my grandmother's house. It was a place I often played, and water ran through it.

One day, while lying on my back across a large rock in the creek, another 'light' spoke to me. This light sparkled down through the treetops, much like the sun, but as I watched it, a strange yet peaceful feeling came over me. My senses sharpened, and I felt a deep sense of connection. I was not alone.

The light spoke to me telepathically. It told me I was loved and held by the whole earth and the stars. It said I always could ask for help when I needed it. It would end up being a moment that defined my belief in the Divine and the Holy for the rest of my life. It also established my deep bond with nature.

In the early 90's, I was driving on a dark country road in Western Pennsylvania late at night. Something internally prompted me to lean forward and look up above the vehicle. What I saw could only be described as a UFO. (And to clarify, I was not under any influence. My child slept in the backseat.) The UFO was slightly wider than the road and flew just above the treetops. It moved as fast as the car, was silent, and had lights that did not shine. I looked at it for several seconds before it darted off to the right and instantly disappeared. It was disorienting, awe-inspiring, and humbling. There is so much we don't know.

In the process of writing this book, I began to see a pattern of inexplicable occurrences in my life. I refuse to believe all such experiences, my own or other people's, are just imaginary delusions. But how do we explain such anomalous things? What do we do with such "hard to explain" encounters? In my life, I often write them down or make visual art to honor them.

Janelle Hardy, a writer and somatic healer, speaks about the "bodypsyche," something I might call our inner wisdom or intuitive body. It is the corporeal, soulful part of us that is beyond our rational, cognitive way of knowing. Hardy says, "It's the part that leads us toward a desire to make meaning out of our life stories – to write, to seek healing, to tend toward the mythic."

Eighteen years ago, I delivered a sermon titled "Making-Meaning," and I talked about our human capacity to do so. I don't think it is make-believe. I think it is more about depth of spirit. I believe this is the part of ourselves we must trust and follow when the mysterious meets the mundane.

As I entered my sixties, a significant truth began to settle: *our time on this planet is not endless, and what matters most deserves my attention.* Returning to my love of art and writing, my lifelong relationship with all things liminal and ethereal, and this story in particular felt less like a decision and more like an acceptance of something that always has been there, patiently waiting for me. It has felt like a kind of *coming home* to myself.

I began to trust that when I authentically put something out into the world, especially in a creative form, it can serve as a kind of beacon attracting others of like mind and heart. I came to realize that we find our tribe, and while our creations might not be for everyone, they will be of importance to someone. I began to trust my own lived experience. In time, I decided to share the fairies' story with a wider audience, and this book began to take shape in my mind.

At first, I thought it might be just a small self-published booklet, but I discovered the book, itself, had other ideas. The story became a kind of ritual of remembrance and reverence, transformational and grounding. It became a symbolic container for a journey between worlds: between fairies and humans, nature and humanity, sacred and mundane, past and present, author and reader, and between my younger and older self. It started helping me to integrate and connect events in my life. The story became a living presence.

The nature of this nested narrative mirrors the layered nature of the world in which we live. The characters and setting explore the psychological complexity, emotional nuance, and mercurial aspects that often accompany, not only mystical and magical experiences, but the span of a lifetime in general. At the heart of this book is a true story, a personal encounter that changed my life. The process of writing the story has been its own journey.

In retrospect, as this book has evolved, I've come to see its themes, its movement, and my own place within it more clearly. While this is my story, it also is part of a greater story that is universal. It explores how we navigate the numinous, how story shapes our lives, how nature is alive with meaning, and how memory, imagination, and generational wisdom are carried and transmitted over time.

THE BEGINNINGS OF A BOOK

Thirty years ago, feeling compelled to preserve the details, I wrote down my encounter with the lights in my journal the day it happened. In the days and weeks that followed, I continued to record the unfolding events as they revealed themselves.

Shortly afterward, I was impelled to put it into story form. Two characters appeared and became narrative vessels to tell my story, extensions of my own voice. There was no master plan. The draft was rough. Then, the story, along with the grandmother and granddaughter, were tucked away in a file cabinet for decades.

For a long time, I was reluctant to share my fairy experience with others. I hesitated to openly name it as a true account not because I doubted what happened, but because I knew how harsh the world can be. I didn't want others diminishing it. We often protect what is precious to the heart.

Over the years, I did end up sharing my fairy story with a few close friends. They frequently responded by offering a story about a strange encounter they had experienced in their own lives. In this way, the story didn't demand belief; it created connection. It was about our shared desire to name the unusual, mysterious, or precious moments we usually keep to ourselves.

I've learned that when given a safe space and the slightest invitation, almost everyone has a story of their own to tell about a numinous, uncanny, or ineffable experience. I believe it's important to talk about the mysterious side of life, about the things that are elusive but carry weight in our lives. Telling my story inspired others to do the same. It mattered.

In November of 2024, I joined a class called *Soul Writing* and started revisiting short stories I had written over the years. I began to outline a book idea incorporating various short stories. As I sorted through old writings, poems, and stories, I noticed a clear pattern. Nearly all of my writing, from as early as nine years of age into my sixties, returned again and again to themes of mystical journeys, spiritual healing, archetypal forms, and how to access our interior life and wisdom. Even my poetry and visual artwork reflected this tension of spirit and matter, visible and invisible. Of course, I always had known this about myself, but seeing it all laid out at once brought a new clarity.

During this mining of old material, the fairy story surfaced again. I thought it might be one story among many in the book I was constructing. Then I noticed something: most of the stories were inspired and channeled works of allegory, fable, and metaphorical fiction. This story, however, originally titled *The Fairies' Tale*, stood apart. It was a true account of something that actually had happened to me. It was shimmering with its own energy, and within a few months it had claimed my full attention. It wanted to be its own book.

When I reread *The Fairies' Tale*, I saw it with new eyes and sensed a deeper purpose, not only in the events themselves but in the framework. I realized the grandmother and granddaughter were not merely characters but aspects of my own psyche, and perhaps the collective psyche, as well. Through them, I was able to shape a narrative that felt more relational and more faithful to the lived experience than I could have managed alone. Their layered timelines carried memory, generational wisdom, and the enduring power of oral storytelling.

By late February of 2025, I had joined another writing collective, A *Writing Room*, and it became clear that the story was no longer willing to wait. During a group discussion, a fellow participant simply said, "*Oh, for gosh sake, just do it. Write it as a memoir. Tell your story. Tell it in your own voice.*" The suggestion startled me.

I hadn't thought of this story as a memoir nor had I considered telling it in the first person. Still, in early March of 2025, with some hesitation, I returned to the original draft and began experimenting with this new idea.

That was when something unexpected happened.

The grandmother and granddaughter came alive on the page with renewed energy as if offended by the idea of being written out. I had read about authors who claimed their characters were animated and vocal in the writing process. This intrigued me.

The story suddenly felt as though it was shaping me more than I was shaping it. It was similar to the feeling I've experienced while making visual art over the course of my life. I'd learned to trust the images. They know the way. Creative ideas have a life of their own. In the book, *Big Magic*, by Elizabeth Gilbert, she says, "Ideas are disembodied, energetic life-forms...capable of interacting with us...and they certainly have will." This time, I had to learn to trust the characters and the story they held.

THE IMPORTANCE OF NAMES

One morning the characters informed me they wanted names. It was then I realized I hadn't named them. Why not? Perhaps it was the unrealized importance of their roles or simply a story unfinished.

Half amused, half curious, I played along and asked aloud, "Okay then, what do you want to be called?"

Without hesitation, I heard, in the etheric depths of my mind, the grandmother answer. "Alma." The name sounded warm and grandmotherly. I suddenly felt as if I was not the one in control here (reminding me of the fairy experience itself.) I was delighted by this reveal.

So, I started to ask, "Well, then what is the granddaughter's name?" but before I could fully form the question, I heard the voice of the granddaughter declaring her name. "My name is Kaiah, pronounced K-eye-ah, with a soft "K" and a gentle "ah" at the end."

The hair on my neck stood up. I was charmed and amused. The voices were distinct. The names were endearing. There was no mistaking it. They were here to stay. I embraced the idea of memoir and let go of my first-person voice. The two story-weavers had it covered.

Although I had no prior familiarity with either name, they felt ancient and new all at once. I long have believed that naming is sacred work. Names carry vibration. The sounds, the syllables, and the way they shape themselves in the mouth all hold meaning.

I intuitively sensed Alma was not the grandmother's given name (I somehow knew her given name was Amanda, although it is never mentioned in the story.) Alma is a name of affection chosen by Kaiah.

When I researched the name Alma, I discovered it means *soul, nourishing, kind, life-giving*. It is also the root of "alma mater," meaning *nourishing mother*. The name Kaiah carries meanings such as *pure, person of the earth, little wise one*, and *new beginning*. Together, they had named themselves well. The resonance felt unmistakable. This revealed something essential about the story itself, about how it wished to be told, and how it wanted to be received.

Together, these characters brought the story to life in a way that speaks to parts of me, and perhaps to parts of you, that often awaken when we encounter the inexplicable. They speak to the parts we need to call upon and trust when we are in the presence of the unknown and unknowable: our inner child and inner wise one. They help us navigate the mystic realms.

Just days later, my husband, knowing I was working on the manuscript, said, "*Happy Anniversary.*"

I was confused because our anniversary was still a month away.

"*It's the thirtieth anniversary of the day your story began,*" he said. It was March 13th, 2025. The realization stunned me. Exactly thirty years had passed.

I felt almost giddy, as if the story had been quietly hibernating all these years and had chosen its own moment to awaken. On its thirtieth anniversary, the characters named themselves, and life rearranged itself so I finally could bring this story into the world. It also was the day the book renamed itself: *In the Company of Fairies: An Unconventional Memoir.*

GRANDMOTHERS AND FAIRIES

It is only with the heart that one can see rightly;
what is essential is invisible to the eye.
~ Antoine De Saint-Exupéry

In January of 2026, as I was doing some research for a later chapter in this book on fairy lore, I discovered a little documentary called *The Fairy Faith* created by John Walker in 2000 in collaboration with the National Film Board of Canada.

'Grandmothers' featured prominently in the stories told. This caught my attention because of how Alma, a grandmother herself, shares her story with Kaiah. I thought it was a sweet connection.

The film begins by John telling his viewers it was his grandmother who inspired his interest in fairies. As the film goes on, another guest, named Peter Aziz, from Devon, England, reveals it also was his grandmother who taught him how to see fairies.

Later in the film, when John meets with a Scottish/Gaelic storyteller named Dolina Wallace, Dolina makes a point to say, "When your grandmother told you that fairies were real, she was telling the truth and wanted to add another dimension to your life – a gift from your grandmother to you."

Near the end of the film, a woman named Murdena Marshall, a Mi'kmaq elder and scholar from Cape Breton, Nova

Scotia, who reportedly photographed fairies in a cave says, "It is easy to call it superstition if you are seeing with your head. You must *see with the heart* and then it is no longer superstition. It becomes belief."

At the end, John reflects back to himself, "Maybe that is what my grandmother was trying to teach me – to believe in your imagination and to see with your heart. It changes how you look at the world."

The threads running through the film all felt uncannily familiar, mirroring the teachings embedded in my own story from thirty years ago. It felt like this film, created twenty-six years ago, was speaking directly to me at a time when I was feeling uncertain about sharing my story at all. After working on my book for almost a year, it felt like an encouraging synchronicity, a confirmation. It was part of a larger story, and I should see this project through.

It mirrored the idea of the archetypal grandmother as a keeper of wisdom and oral tradition, an elder who blesses imagination rather than correcting it, and who lives comfortably with ambiguity.

It made me love the character of Alma all the more.

THE GIFT OF EXCHANGE

Today, as I write, it happens to be March 13, 2026. One year has passed since I began this book in earnest. It is the 31st anniversary of the day I met the fairies. I spent today reading the final draft for this book, noticing how this project took over my life and reflecting on the gifts I have received because of it.

Today, I also learned anthropologists maintain that the span of about thirty-years marks a human generation. In that span perspectives shift and experiences that once seemed confusing or unfinished begin to find their place within the larger story of a life. This got me to thinking about the thirty years it took to write this book.

When I first wrote about Alma, the grandmother, in 1995 I could only imagine the insight of someone twice my age relaying this story. Looking back across that generational arc now, it feels right that I would return to this story and bring it to fruition only after growing into her vantage point. Time has flown.

Fairy lore tells us that the Fair Folk are said to dislike debts. Exchanges are preferred. In many traditional stories, interactions between humans and fairies involve some form of exchange: favors, gifts, offerings, kindness returned. Gifts given should be answered in kind so the balance and connection between worlds is maintained.

I think the writing of this book may be part of an exchange I didn't realize until now, a way of mirroring or completing what began so long ago. Was the impulse to share the story my exchange to the fairies for a glimpse into their realm? OR has the making of this book, and what it has meant to me, been a gift given to me by the fairies in exchange for my help? Are the mirrored and magical elements actually the fairies' own signature on these pages? It is, of course, hard for me to say anything for certain.

As my part in writing this book comes to a close, I have a strange feeling of returning to my true self. Has the act of writing this book restored the balance somehow? Is it a cycle completed? Today it feels as if I have fulfilled something a long time in the making.

Recently, I came to learn that in ancient folklore the beech tree, a central element in this story, has long been associated with knowledge, books, and the written word. It feels fitting that this memoir now rests on paper. What began as a strange and luminous moment in the woods has slowly found its way into creative language. What began in nature has been written back into the earth in a new form. And with it, I find myself grounded again in my realm, at peace, officially returned.

Lori L. Sweet
March 13, 2026

PART IV:

A LIVING CONVERSATION

Remain sitting at your table and listen. Don't even listen. Simply wait, be quiet, still and solitary. The world will freely offer itself to you to be unmasked, it has no choice, it will roll in ecstasy at your feet.
~ Franz Kafka (1883-1924) Jewish Novelist

READER REFLECTIONS

Stories are the creative conversion of life itself into a more powerful, clearer, more meaningful experience.

~ Robert McKee

A teacher and group facilitator at heart, I had to include a space for interactive and reflective explorations. This section offers space for you, dear reader, to pause and reflect on your part of the story, should you wish to do so. It allows the story to breathe and invites you to explore your thoughts and experiences on your own or with others. Within this section you will find prompts for journaling, pondering, storytelling, or group discussion.

Please do not feel that you are meant to answer all of these questions (or any of them). Instead, you may wish to trust your intuition or allow one or two questions to call to you or to guide a group discussion.

PROMPTS FOR REFLECTION & GROUP DISCUSSION

1. Moments That Linger:
Pause. Notice what has stayed with you from the story.

- What feelings stayed with you after finishing the story?

- Was there a particular part of the story that resonated with you or lingered in your mind? What was it, and why might that be?

- How might this story invite you to notice the world differently?

- If you could ask Alma one question, what would it be? How might she answer you?

2. Stillness, Practice, and Joy:
Reflect on what nourishes and sustains you.

- How do you make space for stillness, observation, or listening in your daily life?

- What spiritual or contemplative practices do you nurture? How do you experience the benefits of these practices, and where did you learn them?

- What brings you joy?

3. Nature, Wonder, and Connection:
Notice how the natural world touches you.

- Are there places in nature that feel sacred or especially meaningful to you? What are they and why?

- How does the natural world shape your understanding of wonder, presence, or belonging?

- What ways do you engage with nature? (Gardening, walking, feeding the birds, swimming?)

- Do you feel it is healing or helpful to spend time in nature? Why?

4. Relationships, Love, and Support: *Consider the people and moments that shaped you.*

- Was there an adult in your childhood who inspired or supported you? Who was it? What wisdom, safety, or encouragement did that person offer that influences you today?

- Has someone ever held space for your wonder, curiosity, or mysterious experiences? Who was it? What did that feel like?

- How do you define love? Where do you feel love working in your life?

> *"This story invites you to listen, imagine, and reflect on your own inexplicable moments. Perhaps you, too, have sensed the presence of something unseen: a dream, a whisper in the woods, a quiet moment that subtly shifted your sense of reality. You may have hesitated to trust these experiences or to share them for fear of what others might think. Yet in my experience, when people feel safe enough to share, nearly everyone carries an uncanny or mysterious story of their own. These moments, often quiet, heartfelt, and uncelebrated, inform and shape us even when they resist explanation. They simply matter."* ~ Lori Sweet

5. Intuition, Guidance, and Mystery:

Reflect on unseen guidance and your inner knowing.

- Have you ever experienced something you could not fully explain or prove, but it felt deeply real?

- Have you ever felt guided by something unseen, such as an intuition, a presence, or an inner knowing?

- Have you ever experienced a moment of synchronicity or meaningful coincidence? What made it feel significant to you?

- Do you believe guidance can come from sources we cannot fully name or explain? (Ancestors, Angels, Spirit Guides, God, Spirits, or Muses, etc.) Why or why not?

6. Belief, the Unseen, and Other Realities:
Explore your relationship with what cannot always be seen or named.

- What are your beliefs about fairies, nature spirits, angels, or unseen realms?

- Have you ever had a supernatural, otherworldly, spiritual, or mysterious visitation or experience? What do you remember about it?

- Do you believe we live in a multi-dimensional universe in which our human experience is only one reality that exists? Why or why not?

- Have you ever experienced something that felt mystical, surprising, or quietly transformative while in nature? What happened?

*Have you ever noticed how something profound
happens when we relate stories that matter deeply
to us? Such moments can bring healing and delight.
They help us be more authentic, more in tune with
the deeper rhythms of life.*
~ Maggie Hamilton, Author

EMBODIED PRACTICES

It's not what you look at that matters, its what you see.

~ Henry David Thoreau

This chapter offers some optional embodied activities for you to explore some of the themes in the story, should you wish to do so.

I've spent much of my life guiding others through experiences that awaken creativity, presence, and connection to nature. In my professional work, I've created workshops and practices that help people explore these themes in playful, artistic, and enriching ways.

The exercises that follow are offered in that same spirit. Each one builds on the one before, but each also may be explored on its own. For anyone who wishes to engage with them further, these practices are invitations, and you are welcome to adapt them in whatever way feels right for you.

BREATHWORK: QUIETING THE MIND

Breathing accompanies us from our first moment in this world to our last. Our lungs instinctively take in oxygen and release carbon dioxide, sustaining life without conscious effort. And yet, breath is more than a biological process. It is also a bridge between body and mind, emotion and awareness, the seen and the unseen.

Across many traditions, breath is considered sacred. It is always available - a quiet and free companion that can help settle the nervous system, steady the mind, deepen rest, and awaken subtle awareness within and around us. By learning to work gently with the breath, slowing it, softening it, and allowing it to deepen, we can invite calm presence, and listening.

Practice

Find a comfortable seated position or lie down. Place your hands on your belly. As you breathe in, notice whether your breath moves into the belly, allowing your hands to gently rise, or if the breath stays higher in the chest. If you notice the chest rising, try to relax it and allow the breath to move down into the belly, gently expanding the belly and lower ribs.

Breathe in through your nose and exhale fully through your mouth. Do this for four to six breaths.

Then begin to mentally count as you inhale, slowing the inhalation to a count of four. Pause for a count of one. Exhale slowly to a count of six or eight. Once the exhale is complete, pause again for a count of one.

You may choose to inhale through the nose and exhale through either the nose or the mouth. Continue for four to eight rounds, allowing the mind to settle naturally, without effort.

SENDING AND RECEIVING ENERGY

The world is made of energy. Our bodies generate electrical, magnetic, and thermal processes, and research has shown that the heart itself emits a measurable energetic field. Many traditions have long understood that living beings respond not only to physical care, but also to attention, presence, and intention.

In this practice, choose a living plant, either a houseplant or one growing outdoors. Avoid cut flowers. Find a quiet time when you can sit undisturbed.

Practice

You may begin by greeting the plant or briefly explaining what you are about to do, or you may simply begin.

Start by taking a few slow, deep breaths. You might choose to begin with the breathwork practice offered earlier.

Bring your attention fully to the plant. Using all of your senses, begin to familiarize yourself with it. Look closely. Notice the shape of the leaves, any buds or flowers, the texture of the stems, the colors and variations. Observe the soil. Do you see roots near the surface? Can you sense how old the plant might be?

You may gently touch the plant. Are the leaves smooth, rough, soft, or jagged? You might smell the leaves or the soil. If you have water nearby, take a sip yourself and then offer some to the plant, noticing how the water moves and settles.

Once you feel connected, become quietly receptive. Listen inwardly. You might gently ask the plant if it has any wisdom or message for you. Notice any thoughts, images, sensations, or feelings that arise, without forcing meaning.

Then place your hands near the plant. Bring awareness to your heart center. Sense warmth or subtle movement there. Imagine this gentle energy flowing down through your arms and out through your palms. Offer it to the plant with care and appreciation.

Remain here for two to five minutes. If you sense the plant offering energy back to you, simply receive it with gratitude.

When the practice feels complete, take a deep breath and thank the plant before you depart.

AN EXERCISE IN PRESENCE

Although the human world has separated itself from the natural world in many ways, our bodies remain deeply attuned to it, much as our ancestors once were. When we walk on the earth, away from concrete, noise, and artificial light, our nervous system often settles. Stress hormones and blood pressure can lower. Our thoughts may begin to clear. Intuition and creativity tend to awaken.

You may have heard of practices such as grounding (being barefoot on the earth), or Japanese forest bathing, both known for their restorative effects. No special practice is required. Simply being in nature without electronics and distraction offers its healing balm.

This exercise can be done in your backyard, at a local park, along a beach, or during a walk in the woods. Find a time of at least fifteen minutes when you can be undisturbed. You may do this practice sitting still or while walking.

Practice

Begin by taking a few intentional breaths to settle yourself. Internally state your intention to connect with the natural world. Before you begin, briefly notice how you are feeling mentally, emotionally, and physically, simply taking a quiet inventory.

If you are willing and able, you may remove your shoes and place your bare feet on the earth. If you have not been barefoot outdoors for a long time notice how this changes your awareness of your body in relationship to the earth. You might touch grass, stone, sand, or even the edge of a stream or lake. If removing your shoes does not feel appropriate or possible, the practice is still effective.

Using your senses, notice what is around you. This is an exercise in observation that gently leads to expanded awareness and connection.

Sight: Soften your gaze. Allow what you see to come into your vision without focusing too hard. Become aware of your peripheral vision. Notice colors, shapes, the landscape, the sky. You might also notice negative space, such as the shapes formed by the sky between tree branches. (If you ever looked at "Magic Eye" images, you may recall how shifting your gaze allowed a hidden image to appear.) As your awareness widens, you may begin to sense more than what is immediately visible.

Sound: Listen to the sounds around you. Birds, wind, water, insects, distant voices, or passing cars. If you are walking, notice how sounds change as you move. What feels close? What feels far away?

Smell: Notice any scents. Flowers, soil, leaves, water, or the air itself.

Touch: If you are sitting, touch the ground, the grass, or a nearby tree. If you are walking, you might rest your hand on tree bark or pick up a stone and notice its weight and texture.

If you wish, you may record your experience afterward by writing or drawing. You might sketch a leaf, a stone, or a detail that caught your attention.

When the practice feels complete, pause and notice how you feel now compared to when you began.

CREATIVITY: DRAWING THE SPIRIT OF A TREE

Drawing and making art can be a way to tap into your inner world and the world around you. Often, we think of art as reproducing what we see with our eyes. My artwork is more intuitive and nuanced. I create images that suggest energetic realities and mystical themes. Surrealists, Cubists, and Abstract artists, for example, explore dimensions beyond what we see physically. Visual art is a wonderful way to express what words sometimes cannot.

In this exercise, you are invited to find a favorite tree—perhaps in your yard, your neighborhood, or a nearby wooded area. All you need is a piece of paper and a pencil. You also may use other materials such as a sketchbook, watercolor paper, pastels, crayons, watercolors, or any medium you enjoy. Keep it simple. Think of this as a form of creative journaling; you are not producing work for anyone else. You simply are exploring and expressing for yourself.

Practice

Find your tree and settle at a comfortable distance. Take a few calming breaths to center yourself. You might spend a few moments simply being with the tree, noticing its presence, sending it energy from your heart, or using your senses to feel connected.

Once you feel present, begin to imagine the spirit of the tree, the energy within it. What is its personality? Is it young or old? How does it feel to be near it?

Begin to draw. You do not need to reproduce the tree realistically. Instead, allow your imagination to guide you. Perhaps your tree is bright red and pink with butterflies for leaves. Perhaps you see water and nutrients flowing through the trunk as blue and purple wavy lines. Let the tree's energy, movement, and personality guide your colors, shapes, and lines.

Be playful. Experiment. Be curious. There are no mistakes. This is your personal expression, a reflection of your connection with the tree, your intuition, and the tree's own energies you notice.

When you feel complete, pause and notice how you feel. Perhaps you sense the tree differently now, or perhaps you've discovered something about your own creative voice, your attention, or your connection with life around you.

Finally, you might want to ask the tree if it has a message for you. You might be surprised!

PART V:

EXPANDING THE VIEW

We have idolized the scientific method and the rational process to such a degree that anything trying to speak to us from the irrational or the symbolic is easy to ignore. It also makes us uneasy with its persistent way of appearing at the edges of our awareness like shadow presences that flit in the corners of our eyes but disappear as soon as we look directly at them.

— Jacob Nordby, Author

THREADS OF CONNECTION

*Mystery creates wonder, and wonder is the basis of
our desire to understand.*

~ Neil Armstrong

T hat morning in 1995, as I tried to define what I was seeing,
the lights in the woods told me *"You would call us fairies."*
Therefore, fairies, respectfully, is what I call them. However,
exactly "what fairies are" is a rather complex subject.

In retrospect, I now wish I had asked other questions:
What is your true name? What do you call yourselves? But such
questions are never to be answered. (Some legends say that to
know the true name of a supernatural being grants power over
it. (Think ~ Rumpelstiltskin of the Brothers Grimm.)

As I began writing this book, I felt drawn to broaden my
understanding and to seek the perspectives of those who had
studied fairy lore more deeply. Although I owned hundreds
of books, I discovered I did not own a single one on fairies.
My search for relevant books began late in 2025. I quickly

discovered that fairy lore is vast, contradictory, and endlessly strange.

As my humble explorations unfolded, I found myself wandering into unexpected territories of folklore, sociology, and myth. Relevant information began to surface and my connection to it was visceral. Familiar threads began to appear between my experience and the long human history of encounters with mysterious beings. Other threads, new and unwieldy, wrapped around my imagination in a way that brought new insights and more questions than answers. Let me share a few of the threads I chased.

Irish Touch

One of those threads led me into Irish folklore and fairy lore, traditions I knew little about when I began. Thinking back to my own encounter, it occurred to me that the woman who assisted me at the festival was Irish. She had been speaking about fairies in Ireland and Britain. I began to wonder if the Irish beliefs held more relevance than I originally understood. I also began to wonder if the man I had assumed was a Christian monk might have been something else entirely, perhaps an ancient Druid or Celtic priest.

And Jason (not his real name, though he was a real person) was Scottish. These retrospective discoveries feel to me like playful clues, the kind that have appeared at other times in my life, reminding me to pay attention: *There is more going on than meets the eye.*

Water Ways

Recently, water has captured my attention in a more mystical way. I've come to realize how the water element has long appeared in my night-time dreams, artwork, astrology, and (unfortunately) recurring patterns of home repair projects. It feels as though it wants my attention. Exploring the deeper roles water plays in the universe and in my own life is an ongoing meditation these days.

In fairy lore, water is profoundly relevant, serving not only as a dwelling place for the Fair Ones, but also as a boundary, a source of power, and a portal or doorway between our world and theirs. Discovering water's connection to fairies feels like another piece of my puzzle.

I was near water the day I saw the lights, and it was raining the day I moved the fairies. Did water serve as a gateway between realms? Was the water more significant than I had realized? It is intriguing to speculate.

Tree Medicine

During my research, I learned the Celtic tradition considers the oak to be the King of the Forest. On a whim, I typed into a search bar, *If the oak is the king of the forest, who is the queen?* The answer? The beech tree. Beech trees are described, in some traditions, as magical places where fairies dwell.

It never occurred to me to question why Jason and I ended up at a beech tree that day. This felt relevant. As this realization seeped into my awareness, it seemed as though the deeper threads of the story were continuing to reveal themselves.

As Queen or Mother of the Forest, the beech was seen as a source of nourishment, shelter, and good fortune. It long has been associated with wisdom, knowledge, and writing. Interestingly, the Old English words for beech and book may share linguistic roots. Perhaps the beech tree was foretelling this book all those many years ago.

Learning about ancient and modern fairy stories has been an adventure in itself. The more I learn the more curious I become about why these beings have followed humanity for so long. Why are there so many encounters reported around the world and across generations? What might that mean for all of us?

I can't prove that fairies are real, but the people who tell stories about fairies are real and there are, to my enjoyment, quite a few of them. I came to see that my story was only one story within a larger collective, part of a continuum of supernatural, paranormal, and mysterious experiences woven throughout human history.

In his 1917 book, *The Idea of the Holy*, Rudolf Otto, a German Lutheran theologian, coined the term "the numinous" from the root word 'numen' to denote an emotional state of consciousness receptive to receiving spiritual or otherworldly insight. Otto's famous phrase, "*Mysterium tremendum et fascinans*," means a mystery that can be overwhelming or even unsettling but is equally awe-inspiring and fascinating. It is beyond rational explanation. While Otto was not speaking directly about fairies, I believe his description is quite fitting as we enter their realm of wonder.

FAIRY LORE

*If thou thinkest that thou understandest and know-
est much; yet know that there be many more things
which thou knowest not.*
  ~ Thomas à Kempis, German-Dutch Monk

The material here is not meant to be exhaustive. There are extensive volumes written on fairies, folklore, and the supernatural. I'm not a folklorist nor is this an academic study of fairy lore. What follows is simply a gathering of ideas and stories that stirred my own curiosity while writing this book. I have provided a Sources and Resources section at the end if you wish to explore further on your own.

While the following material may at times seem disorienting or overwhelming, my desire is to avoid unintentionally attempting to domesticate something that is, I believe, by its very nature, untamable.

WHAT'S IN A NAME?

In 1995, as a woman in the United States, I spell the word "fairy" the way I learned it: f-a-i-r-y. For many of us, this name refers to a cute little nature spirit or flower fairy who is a small human-like being with wings, made familiar to us in tales like Disney's *Peter Pan* and *Fern Gully: The Last Rainforest*. We wouldn't be wrong, of course, but such fairies are a modern expression of a much larger and older story.

There are older spellings such as Faerie, Fairie, and Fae and other form of the name that share roots across languages: the German *Fee*, Latin *Fata* (fate), Norwegian *Fe*, Russian *Feya*, and Old English *Fey*.

When I decided to do a little research into the world of fairies, I had no idea this simple word could send me into such a wonderland of strange origin stories and definitions. I have come to learn "fairy" is not the name of one kind of entity but rather envelops a vast diversity of supernatural/paranormal beings with similar characteristics, reported by humans throughout different lands and over time.

While globally recognizable, the term fairy is not universally defined, and, in a strange way, the world seems content with that. As I discovered, there is something about all things "fairy" that is evasive, elusive, and mercurial. This global embrace of "fairy," without definitive meaning, speaks of a deeper level of trust and knowing that defies reason, yet it resonates with the human heart and imagination across barriers.

As I continued reading, I was surprised to learn that the word *faerie* did not originally refer to a tiny winged being or any specific beings at all. In its earliest forms it was associated with enchantment, fate, and even a hidden realm or world rather than a distinct race of creatures. Only later, in the 14th-16th centuries, did the term begin to attach itself to the inhabitants of the Otherworld.

In some places, particularly in Ireland and Britain, it was considered improper, even dangerous, to name fairies directly. Instead, people used respectful titles: *The Fair Folk, The Wee Ones, The Good People, The People of the Mounds, The Other Crowd, and The Gentry.* These were not simply creative substitutes; they reflected a lived and negotiated relationship. The connection was intimate, tied to land, life, and death. Like wary neighbors, it was vital to remain in their favor through belief, gifts, and proper address.

There are other names as well, each carrying its own history and beliefs. In Ireland, the Sidhe (shee) are an ancient race believed now to live in the land itself. In Wales, the Tylwyth Teg (The Fair Family), a class of fairies, are said to move between the human world and their own unseen domains. Similar supernatural beings appear in strikingly different forms around the world: nature spirits such as the Finnish Haltia, Brazilian Curupira, Iroquois Jogah, Greek Dryads, and the Japanese Kodama. And then there are the figures many of us recognize more readily from fairy tales and folklore such as elves, mermaids, selkies, banshees, brownies, devas, pixies, and trolls. Our cute little, winged garden companions are not alone!

There is a staggering amount of history, story, and terminology devoted to them all and yet uncertainty, paradox, and mystery continue to surround them. Perhaps this ambiguity is simply part of their nature. What we call "fairy" is less a fixed name and more like shifting sands that expand, contract, and reshape themselves.

Even so, the relevance of their appearance in human experiences and stories remains. The very idea of fairies, real or imagined, is woven into the human landscape, shaping culture and our engagement with the unseen world.

WHAT IS A FAIRY?

*To see a faery one must learn to "see" with the heart
and the mind as well as with the eyes.*
~ Edain McCoy, Author

So, what is a fairy? That sounds like a question that should have a simple answer, but defining a fairy is a surprisingly difficult task. It is possible the word fairy has become a bit of a catch-all term for any uncanny thing we encounter and fail to understand. It is possible that, rather than being a single kind of entity, fairy/faerie really is a term that holds a diverse collective of supernatural beings that have populated our lands and imaginations for generations.

The Oxford English dictionary defines a fairy as "*one of a class of supernatural beings of diminutive size, in popular belief, supposed to possess magical powers.*" This definition fits our modern imagination that often pictures fairies as small, winged beings who are magical caretakers of the earth.

While this image may have its own merits, historically it became popular during the Victorian era through theatre portrayals and romantic literature and art. Older European folklore offers a much different picture.

ANCIENT AND TRADITIONAL FAIRIES

The pagan folk of old Europe described faeries as human-like and wingless, often smaller than humans, though they also could be human-sized or larger. It was believed they had the ability to interact with humans from a dimension embedded within our own. They married, had babies, worked, made music, and were deeply connected to the land. Communities of fairies lived near communities of humans, forming relational bonds with people and the landscapes they both shared.

Across centuries and cultures fairies have been seen as agents of enchantment, sometimes playful, sometimes fierce, even life-threatening, reminding us that the world contains forces beyond ordinary sight and understanding.

Alive, social, morally complex, and intimately connected to the flow of life, they occupied (and still occupy) a liminal space: both familiar and unknowable, a living presence that persists in human imagination and experience.

These traditional fairies had their own laws, cultures, and ceremonies. They were territorial and morally ambivalent, capable of great kindness, mischief, or even cruelty and they were/are remarkably human in their complexity. They were not the modern conception of nature spirits nor abstract elemental forces, but a fierce social and supernatural community existing alongside human society. (And perhaps they still do.)

Dr. Simon Young, a British historian and folklorist specializing in supernatural beliefs and fairy lore, defines fairies as "social supernatural" beings, differentiating them from entities such as ghosts, and he admits plainly: *"Fairies of today are not the same as fairies two hundred years ago."* What are we to make of this?

Let's dig a little deeper by taking a look at some interesting definitions and theories, both ancient and modern.

In ancient Rome and Greece, long before there were elves or brownies or garden spirits, the unnamed essence we now call fairies was more a personification of our inevitable destiny. In the very ancient echoes of these beliefs the "beings" were left unnamed. They were seen as the collective spirits of the land or the ancestors. They were impersonal forces of the environment that could grant life and death.

In Greek mythology we see the three sisters of fate, the Moirai, the spinners, who spun the threads of life. The English word fairy is derived from the term *fata*, meaning "the fates" in Latin. It embodied a deeper philosophy and cosmology that believed in an ordered universe where forces beyond human control governed life. Destiny was inescapable. Life was interwoven with invisible threads which were seen as the hidden dimensions of the natural world.

As time went on, the terms gradually evolved in medieval Europe to refer to a woman who was an enchantress. A Fay, or enchantress, was a powerful woman, otherworldly or human, innately skilled in magic and prophecy, who appeared at births to declare a child's destiny. (Think Morgan Le Fay)

In the medieval mind there came a time when the line between fairy, enchantress, and witch grew very thin. As the church tightened its grip on older beliefs and practices, there was growing condemnation of magic and all things tied to the power (and unpredictable nature) of nature. These figures, once seen as noble and fate-bound, were increasingly scapegoated and targeted.

During the late medieval and early modern witch trials, many clergy and inquisitors reinterpreted encounters with spirits, including fairie, as demonic deception. Human women who had oracular or healing powers, close association to nature and elementals, or simply were independent women of means were linked to supernatural forces and killed as witches. I wonder if this contributed to the idea of the "enchanted ones" going into hiding where nature's full range of power, both life-giving and destructive, could be expressed without fear.

In early medieval Ireland (6th–8th Century), another origin story developed that spoke about the Aos Sí (Shee), the People of the Mound, who were said to descend from an ancient race called the Tuatha Dé Danann, the divine beings of Irish mythology. The mythology belongs to the older Gaelic cultural world that included both Ireland and parts of Scotland.

The Tuatha De Danann were believed to be a radiant and powerful race who possessed immense magic. After being defeated in battle by the ancestors of the human Celts, they withdrew from the visible world, retreating into the earth and into an unseen realm that came to be known as the Otherworld.

They were said to dwell within hollow hills and ancient mounds, places where the veil between worlds was thin. One such place is Sìthean Mòr (the Big Fairy Hill) on the Isle of Iona in Scotland where the Sidhe are believed to live within the mountain itself. The Isle of Iona long has been considered a "thin place," where the boundary between the human world and the Otherworld is especially permeable. It's where the presence of the unseen and the fairies still can be felt in the land.

It is important to note that nothing exists in a vacuum. Historical and cultural shifts impact all facets of life and belief. Christian doctrine and the scientific inquiry of the Renaissance began to change how humans saw themselves in the universe. The Enlightenment and the industrialization of the modern era continued to reinforce beliefs in human power over nature. How did these views change our relationship with the land and with the world of Faerie?

With the spread of Christian influence in Iona and throughout the Celtic lands, another theory emerged. This was the theory of the fallen angels. According to this belief, during the war in Heaven, there were angels who chose neither to side with God nor Satan, but remained neutral. For their indecision, they were cast down and condemned to dwell in the in-between realms of the earth. Over time, these fallen ones became associated with the Fair Folk.

What interests me about this theory is that it doesn't entirely deny the existence of fairies but rather reinterprets them through a Christian lens. They became understood not as supernatural pagan beings, but as diminished angels. In this way, perhaps, the old beliefs were not entirely erased but redefined, allowing the people to continue believing in the presence of fairies while remaining within the boundaries of an increasingly Christian world. As mentioned earlier, however, not all Christian leaders sympathized and faeries were demonized and feared through this lens as well.

One source I came across described the Sidhe/Tuatha De Danann as tall, elegant beings with pointed ears, cat-like eyes, and luminous skin. This conjured up images of aliens depicted from UFO encounters. I began to wonder if these "gods" were actually an advanced alien race, with technologies interpreted at that time as divine powers. I thought I might be really out there with this one until my research led me to The Extraterrestrial Hypothesis (ETH).

The ETH does, in fact, propose that the folklore of the Sidhe or Tuatha De Danann were possibly ancient misinterpretations of visits from advanced alien civilizations. I found this interesting. Additionally, there is similarity in the many stories told about humans abducted by fairies that mirror stories of present-day alien abductions.

> So, the reality of Fairies – if fairies are real– must be of a kind that allows for illusions, deceptions, and seeming impossibilities.
>
> ~ Jeremy Harte, Author

I soon discovered yet another perspective, one that refuted ETH. Jacques Vallée, computer scientist and author of *Passport to Magonia*, proposes that UFOs and aliens are not extraterrestrial visitors at all, but rather a modern manifestation of an intelligent, interdimensional force present in creation here on earth. This force, Vallée explains, has interacted with humanity throughout history, appearing as fairies, demons, or angels. Vallée rejects the ETH because he believes the phenomenon's behavior is more consistent with a force that exists alongside our dimension rather than aliens traveling from other planets.

NATURE FAIRIES

While people of literate cultures often speak about the natural world, indigenous, oral people often speak directly to that world, acknowledging certain animals, plants, and landforms as expressive subjects with whom they might find themselves in conversation.

~ David Abram, Becoming Animal

There is yet another entirely different group of theories that speak about "fairies" as guardians of the earth, nature spirits, and spirits of natural phenomena.

Paracelsus, known as the father of toxicology, lived during the German Renaissance in the late fifteenth and early sixteenth centuries. He famously categorized fairies as elementals: Undines/water, Sylphs/air, Gnomes/earth, Vulcani/fire. They were, to Paracelsus, personifications of nature, or rather beings without souls that helped plants to grow and weather to form. This was a significant shift from earlier fairy beliefs.

Centuries later, during the Victorian age (1837-1901), artists and writers increasingly portrayed fairies as tiny, whimsical, and winged creatures, an image familiar to the modern world.

The story of Sleeping Beauty offers one illustration of these changing perceptions over time. In the early tale *Sun, Moon, and Talia,* by Giambattista Basile (1634), slumber and curses resulted from fate, destiny, and prophecy. Reminiscent of the *fata*, they were forces beyond human control rather than magical beings with agendas. In 1697, Charles Perrault introduced fairies as powerful enchantresses who would bestow gifts or curses in his version, *Sleeping Beauty in the Wood*.

By 1959, Disney transformed these beings into small, winged "fairy godmothers" with distinct personalities who served as guardians of children against the evil fairy, Maleficent. Their names, Flora, Fauna, and Merryweather, hint at the aspects of nature these beings influenced. The ancient fates changed form into figures of personality and magic who stood at the thresholds of destiny and chance, life and death.

Alongside the Victorian romantics there came Theosophy, an esoteric movement established around 1875 led by figures such as Helena Blavatsky. In this tradition fairies were thought to belong to the Deva Kingdom and were the architects of nature. Such nature spirits were assigned to specific flowers or trees or phenomena of nature. The Theosophists did not see fairies as supernatural beings, but rather, they believed they were made of etheric matter and were vibrations of energy that could be visible to clairvoyant humans with second sight while being invisible to the normal human eye.

> *We can't hear a dog whistle or see rays coming out of cell phones. There are lots of things that we know exist in our world and we can't see them. Why should fairies be any different?*
>
> ~ Signe Pike, Author

Eileen Kigran, in her 2009 article, *Fairies and Faeries*, says that fairies arrived long before humans and remain part of the earthly architecture. She claims fairies are young nature spirits and energetic beings of light doing loving service. As they grow older, they become Devas and sustain life on this planet. Kirgran's ideas are echoed in the work of Samuel B. Lee, a contemporary spiritual teacher who integrates psychiatry and quantum physics in his work.

In his 2025 YouTube video called *"The Hidden Race Keeping Earth Alive,"* Lee says, "Fairies weave sound and light codes into the land which maintains the living balance between earth's energetic body and all biological life, including humans."

There are people and whole communities today that still believe in and promote the reality of fairies in partnership with humans, particularly around the issue of caring for the planet.

Murdena Marshall, a Mi'kmaq elder and scholar from Cape Breton, Nova Scotia, in the documentary, *Fairy Faith,* explains that the "little people" are not just European folklore but are deeply rooted in the Mi'kmaq tradition and the physical landscape of the Maritimes. She discusses fairies as real entities that interact with our world and offers advice to those interested in how to respect and understand them rather than treating them as mere myths.

Findhorn, Scotland, a well-known spiritual community founded in 1962, is associated with miraculous gardening and deep nature connection. The story goes that one of its co-creators, Dorothy Maclean, communicated with devas (the architects) and nature spirits (the craftsmen) on an ongoing basis. She believed they were real and intelligent beings who guided her work with the difficult soil in that location.

Faithfully following this guidance, Findhorn produced unusually large and vibrant plants, drawing international attention at their success. At Findhorn, fairies are seen as intelligent energy forms essential to the growth of the planet. They are active partners in creation.

The Findhorn beliefs include the idea that fairies, as shape shifters, might shape themselves to human expectations, appearing as winged beings if that is what we expect to see in order to speak a visual language we will understand. Their goal is to help us take better care of the home we all share.

> *The form of faeries, like everything else about them, is fluid and changeable... When we encounter fairies, our minds tend to clothe this energy in forms it can understand. ...the fairies' take visible shape in forms derived from location, from our expectations, or from traditional mythic archetypes.*
> ~ Brian Froud, Author & Artist

Returning to the island of Iona briefly, it is interesting to note that the more contemporary small winged fairies (referred to as SWFs by Dr. Simon Young) also have made appearances there. In the book *Seeing Fairies*, one story about a Mrs. Pauline McKay of Glasgow describes several fairy sightings in the early 1950's on Iona. One note read, "Oct 16: I saw a fairy of small angelic form with very blonde hair and two small white wings."

Marjorie T. Johnson (1911–2010), a remarkable figure in the realm of the paranormal, dedicated her life to exploring the existence of fairies and documenting encounters with these elusive beings. She was the secretary of the Fairy Investigation Society (FIS) and meticulously gathered stories about fairy sightings. The stories today can be found in the book, "*Seeing Fairies.*"

Marjorie Johnson believed fairies existed on a different vibrational frequency and were therefore normally invisible to human eyes. However, when a person was receptive or when the fairies desired contact, the veil between the two worlds briefly could lift to allow visibility or interaction. In the book's introduction, Marjorie writes,

> *When the nature spirits wish to materialize at the physical-etheric level in order to be seen more clearly by each other and by certain human beings, they can slow down the rate of their vibrations so that they are on a different wavelength, and when they want to vanish, they increase the vibrations again and so disappear from human sight into a higher dimension.*

As I already have mentioned, the world of fairies is replete with theories that challenge each other and there are some that push back against the idea of fairies as nature spirits or elementals.

John Beckett, in his April 9, 2019 blog article, *Why the Fair Folk Aren't Nature Spirits*, explains that nature spirits are considered part of the natural, human world. They don't move between worlds. They are tied to their element or location, mostly solitary, and don't behave socially like fairies.

Fairies, in contrast, according to Beckett, are otherworldly social creatures in their own right who travel, migrate, marry, live, die, and have babies. If they protect a tree or water way it is because they are defending something they view as their territory. According to Beckett, they are not defenders of nature, cosmic gardeners, nor the spirits of flowers. Beckett doesn't seem to deny the idea of nature spirits, only that they have their own reality, different from fairies.

This all made me think about the fairies I encountered. First of all, I saw them as small lights, but I had the feeling that was not their true form. They had babies and desired to move to a new location. I felt they were connected to the earth, embedded in our world, perhaps in an alternate or parallel world (a different vibrational frequency), and independently alive. I realize I never thought of them as the spirit of the tree itself. I didn't experience them as the scary faeries of old, either. It just seemed to be where they lived. It simply felt as if two worlds touched.

So, how do we make sense of it all? The word "fairy" may serve as a broad umbrella for phenomena that are not identical, such as a mermaid and a troll, yet share certain qualities that allow them to be grouped together.

Humans love to define and categorize everything. For example, we categorize a large number of creatures under terms like "animal" or "mammal," and yet a whale is very different from a mouse. Are our smaller, winged garden fairies related to the older, traditional faeries in some way, or are they something entirely different?

David Boyle, a contemporary British author and researcher who explores the persistence of fairy belief in the modern world, writes, "Just because fairies as nature spirits is a new interpretation doesn't mean it isn't [equally as] true [as older interpretations.]"

I do believe paradox is alive and well in the fairy realms. Two things could be true at the same time. Still, it very well may be that we are dealing with things beyond human understanding, and all we can do is speculate.

In short, nothing has ever been said of fairies in one story that could not be countered by another equally authoritative story to the contrary. Fairies are resistant to all definitions.

~ Jeremy Harte, Author

Fairy tales remind us constantly not to take what we see at face value but to look into the heart of things.

~ Maggie Hamilton, Author

FAIRIES AND THE DEAD

While not talked about as often, there are some origin theories that suggest fairies themselves are spirits of the dead who are trapped in purgatory and sometimes materialize in our world.

This contradicts some folklorists who sees ghosts as non-living, solitary entities, whereas fairies are more often defined in folklore as a living race, just like humans, but in a parallel world. This whole line of thinking got me to wondering what Spiritualists had to say about fairies. Do they believe in them?

When I met my fairies, I lived very close to Lily Dale, the world's largest Spiritualist community founded in the 19th century. Spiritualists and mediums live on the grounds and guest speakers like Barbara Marciniak, Dr. Wayne Dyer, and John Edward have visited their public stage. I visited their grounds on many occasions.

Over time, along a particular path in the woods on the Lily Dale property, people began leaving tiny houses, ornaments, and offerings for the fairies. By 2016, the "Fairy Wing Way" was a well-established enchanted habitat celebrating the fairies of Lily Dale. (I admit, for fun, I left a small fairy statue there myself back in 2008, under a rotting log and frequently visited to leave shiny gifts.)

According to my research, the spiritual community of Lily Dale defines fairies as benign and elemental nature spirits that inhabit the woodlands and coexist with the human spirit world. Fairies, in spiritualist circles, are considered intelligent, conscious, non-corporeal custodians of the woods believed to be part of the otherworldly realms. One source described them as interdimensional beings who live with the spirits of our dead.

Following our pattern of conflicting beliefs, some Spiritualists fear that a belief in fairies discredits their efforts to prove the survival of the human soul after death. Again, there is no full consensus.

FAIRIES AND PSYCHOLOGY

Finally, I have to include the psychological perspective and the theory that fairies are simply projections of our own fears and desires. Many psychological theories claim human encounters are the result of 'some kind of real experience' but reject the idea that fairies are objectively and physically real. Fairies might be manifestations of hallucinations, figments of our imagination, spiritual visions, waking dreams, or, at times, fabrications.

For me, explanations in psychology raise their own questions: What is imagination? What are hallucinations? Are they merely functions of the brain, or could they be doorways into other layers of perception or even another world? Why do human beings have spiritual visions and what are they? What is second sight? Is any of this real? What does "real" even mean?

In the documentary *The Fairy Faith*, Dr. Mark Fox, a British scholar of religion, is interviewed. He studies paranormal and anomalous experiences, especially how humans interpret encounters with the unexplained. He offers a perspective that reflects the complexity of such encounters:

> When we see something paranormal, we often think it either exists objectively outside of ourselves in the physical world, or it doesn't exist. But I am wondering if the realm of the imagination, the realm in which fairies dwell, is in fact an intermediate realm, neither completely in your head nor completely in the world, but somehow

crossing over or transcending the two; belonging to both and yet belonging to neither. That,
of course, is something which many educated,
secular, scientifically trained Westerners find
hard to accept.

Carl Jung (1875–1961) was a Swiss psychiatrist and psy-
choanalyst who founded analytical psychology and often
used dream analysis. He once had a patient who confessed
that he had fabricated his dreams for weeks. Jung said, in
essence, it didn't matter if he fabricated the dreams. What
the patient made up still revealed something true about his
inner world and the nature of the human mind. He believed
the psyche speaks through symbol and archetype whether
the source is internal or external.

FINDING MEANING
IN WHAT REMAINS UNDEFINED

If you think tales about fairies are a thing of the past, you
would be wrong. Dr. Simon Young has been cataloging modern fairy encounters, happening today, through the revived
Fairy Investigation Society (FIS). He publishes 500 stories at
a time in the *Fairy Census* as part of the *Fairy and Folklore
Series*. The stories continue.

I find myself asking questions such as, "Have fairies
evolved over time? Has the 'second sight' of humans changed
over time? Where is the imagination? Does supernatural phenomena change or respond as human needs and culture
change? There are invisible forces proven by science, so what

else might be invisible to us? Are we all talking about the same thing, or is there more than one thing going on here?"

I wish I had the answers. *What fairies are* seems to defy definition. The spectrum of theories of origin reveals the nuances and complexity of this topic.

However, what I find interesting is that all this conflicting information, paradox, and contradiction does not seem to deflect from the deeper questions or beliefs. For believers, this simply does not seem to be a problem. For non-believers, it leaves room for doubt and speculation. For me, it is insanely fascinating.

I have a general sense of my own definition, but words continue to fall short. I mostly imagine fairies as otherworldly beings sharing this earth in a parallel dimension, deeply connected to the land, but not reducible to it. Still, for me, all the theories offer some elements worth contemplating.

> *Animism perceives all things – animals, plants, rivers, human made objects and even words and thoughts as animated, living things.*
> ~ Imelda Almquist, Author

I am struck by the idea that some of our oldest fairy traditions may have emerged from an animistic way of seeing the world, one in which humans understood themselves to be in conversation with the land, the waters, the trees, and the unseen energies and worlds around them. This aligns with many indigenous belief systems, some still held today, and fits within my own cosmology.

Peter Knight said, "I think there are unseen realms that occasionally flicker into our reality. I believe, as humans, we're only seeing a very small part of what actually exists in the universe."
~ as quoted by Signe Pike in Faery Tale

I'm enamored also with the ancient concepts of the spirits of fate and destiny and equally at home with Johnson's focus on vibrational frequencies as gateways between the realms. I can agree with Simon Young, who is careful to note that there is no definitive, universally agreed-upon interpretation.

Fairy belief is a global phenomenon marked by extraordinary diversity. It can be approached historically, spiritually, scientifically, mythologically, anthropologically, psychologically, or sociologically. Each path illuminates something, yet no single path explains everything.

Jo Hickey-Hall, folklorist and creator of The Modern Fairy Podcast said, on her episode June 22, 2022, "*We don't have to come up with the answers, but having the conversations is important.*" I agree with her.

As I wander through these questions, I find myself in good company. Historians and folklorists have been circling this mystery for generations. Simon Young honestly and charmingly admitted in a recent podcast with Jo Hickey-Hall that, after forty years of devotion to the topic, he doesn't know for certain if he knows more now than when he began.

On Michelle Franklin's podcast, *Legends and Lectures* (February 7th 2026), historian Dr. Francis Young, in discussing his deep study for his book *Twilight of the Godlings*, humbly admits that although he set out to untangle the origins of these beings, the deeper he went, the more layered and uncertain the picture became. I find these musings by the scholars strangely reassuring.

Author of the book *Inside the Secret Life of Fairies*, Maggie Hamilton, observed that one of the gifts of fairy encounters is how "the luminosity of a single moment can remain with us, allowing us to draw on its energy and meaning even years later." That sentiment reflects something I understand deeply from my own experiences and the one I share in this book.

Whatever we call them, whatever they are, they matter to human beings. In spite of all the shifting interpretations and undefinable phenomena, something persists. Across centuries and cultures, humans continue to describe encounters with an unseen presence at the edge of the ordinary world. What strikes me most is not the disagreement in theories, it is the persistence of encounters.

Whether they are autonomous beings, nature spirits, archetypes rising from the collective psyche, interdimensional visitors, or luminous inventions of the imagination, they continue to appear in our collective stories and sometimes in our own lives, even when defining or proving any of it remains elusive.

Perhaps the greater task is not settling *what fairies are* but rather acknowledging that the idea and the experiences surrounding them are somehow deeply embedded in the human landscape. Whatever their source, they continue to surface, generation after generation, asking to be witnessed.

Perhaps the difficulty in defining Faerie is not a failure of research but part of its nature. The world of enchantment always has been described as resistant to being pinned down to a single explanation. The more firmly we try to grasp it, the more it slips *sideways* into another form. Maybe that, too, is part of the story.

> *Turn sideways into the light as they say the old ones did and disappear into the originality of it all. Be impatient with easy explanations and teach that part of the mind that wants to know everything not to begin questions it cannot answer.* (Excerpt from Turn Sideways into the Light)
>
> ~David Whyte, Poet

Perhaps the world of enchantment is not meant to resolve itself neatly under examination. Perhaps its mercurial quality, its tendency to blur, merge, contradict, and reform, is not a flaw in our understanding but part of its very character.

Perhaps that is where the mystery will forever dwell, calling to us when the veil is thin, whispering of earth's magic, inevitably touching our lives, hopefully for the better, and then leaving us to the business of living life in our own realm.

May we all be so blessed.

ACKNOWLEDGEMENTS

My deepest gratitude goes to my husband, Tom Sweet, whose unwavering support, encouragement, and patience carried me through this process. Thank you for holding space, for reading and rereading my work so many times, and for believing in me, my creative process, and this story.

I am grateful to the people throughout my life who have embraced the mystical, the spiritual, the ineffable, and the uncanny, and who have been willing to explore alongside me: Kim Robbins, Myron Eshowsky, Michelle Buhite, Tayria Ward, Eileen Tanfani, Marielle Soong, Elizabeth Terry, Lynne Niehaus, Sally Field, and many more. You all are in my heart.

I want to thank my son, Jaymes Thompson, for his wonderfully intelligent and creative mind and for all the ways he has inspired me since he was born through his own mystical experiences and his willingness to ponder them.

I am especially thankful to those who encouraged me to share this story when I was unsure whether I should, particularly Nicole Mills and Peggy McConnel whose gentle reassurances gave me courage. And, thank you to Dorothy Grimm and author, Maggie Hamilton, who both enthusiastically read the final draft for me and cheered.

I'm deeply grateful for A *Writing Room* collective and all the kindness, creativity, knowledge, feedback, technical support, and quiet companionship that is shared there.

My gratitude also goes to Lauren Sapala, whose work and book, *Writing on the Intuitive Side of the Brain*, helped me to understand how my mind works and gave me permission to write this book in my own way.

Thank you to Jennifer Newcomb for her class on book cover design and for her assistance with mine. And to Kari Hultman, thank you for your generous assistance with my publishing logo and images.

Thank you to the Fairy Investigation Society for reminding me that I am not alone and that unexplainable things deserve to be honored with both academic rigor and child-like wonder.

Thank you to the real Jason and Alice (you know who you are) for believing in me when it mattered most. Thank you to the unnamed woman who helped me to remember.

My deep gratitude to Mother Earth for her beauty and gifts and to the quiet, ever-present, other-worldly forces, muses, and spirit helpers who guide and accompany me.

And finally, to the fair ones: you have my respect.

Selected Books & Resources

The following books and resources (in no particular order) were helpful to me this past year as I created the fairy lore section. Some are scholarly works grounded in folklore and historical research, while others present personal experiences, artistic interpretations, speculations, or modern investigations. Together they reflect the wide range of perspectives through which this enduring subject continues to be explored.

This is only a partial list of materials, and by including them I am only offering a starting point for readers if you wish to do your own additional explorations. Many other thoughtful and well-researched works deserve recognition but were beyond the scope of this project.

Enjoy the search!

Scholarly, Historical, and Contemporary Works and Researchers

<u>Marjorie T. Johnson</u>: *Seeing Fairies: From the Lost Archives of the Fairy Investigation Society* ~ A carefully preserved collection of firsthand fairy encounter reports gathered in Britain during the mid-twentieth century by the Fairy Investigation Society.

<u>Simon Young and Ceri Houlbrook</u>: *Magical Folk: British and Irish Fairies, 500 AD to the Present* ~ A comprehensive academic survey tracing fairy belief through historical records, folklore, and modern eyewitness accounts.

<u>Francis Young</u>: *Fairies: A History (Forthcoming book 2026)* ~ A historian's examination of fairy belief from medieval Europe through the modern era, exploring its religious, cultural, and psychological dimensions. Also by Young, *Twilight of the Godlings* ~ Explores how ancient nature spirits and local deities evolved into the fairy traditions preserved in European folklore.

<u>Robert Kirk</u>: *The Secret Commonwealth of Elves, Fauns, and Fairies (1691)* ~ One of the earliest known firsthand theological and folkloric treatises on fairy beings, written by a Scottish minister.

<u>Eddie Lenihan</u>: *Meeting the Other Crowd* ~ An Irish folklorist presents traditional accounts and oral histories from Ireland's rich and enduring fairy traditions.

<u>Morgan Daimler</u>: *Fairies: A Guide to Celtic Fair Folk* ~ A modern synthesis of Celtic folklore and historical sources examining traditional beliefs about fairies.

<u>Katharine Briggs</u>: *The Fairies in Tradition and Literature* ~ A respected folklorist's overview of fairy traditions across European history and literature.

<u>W. B. Yeats</u>: *Fairy and Folk Tales of the Irish Peasantry* (1888) & *The Celtic Twilight* (1893)

<u>The Fairy Investigation Society</u> Originally founded in 1927 to collect and preserve firsthand accounts of fairy encounters, revived in recent years to document contemporary reports. Offers free and purchasable online copies of materials. www. fairyist.com

<u>Jeremy Harte</u>: *Explore Fairy Traditions* ~ A book with detailed exploration of folk traditions, historical beliefs, and contemporary encounters, highlighting how fairy belief has persisted and evolved over time.

<u>Jo Hickey-Hall</u>: ScarletoftheFae.com ~ Website with resources exploring modern fairy encounters, folklore, and research. Jo Hickey-Hall has a forthcoming book expected in 2026, *Modern Fairy Sightings: Personal Encounters in Extraordinary Times*.

First-Person/Experiential Perspectives

<u>Maggie Hamilton</u>: *Inside the Secret Life of Fairies: Where Dreams Come True* ~ A contemporary guide to discovering

fairies, how to communicate with them, and how to work with them to heal the earth and your own heart.

Marcia Zina Mager: *Believing in Faeries: A Manual for Grown-Ups* ~ A gentle, reflective work exploring belief, perception, and personal openness to the unseen world.

Signe Pike: *Faery Tale* ~ A personal memoir describing the author's encounters during a pilgrimage to fairy sites, blending historical context with modern experience.

David Spangler: "The Sidhe and the Guardian Exercise," *Quest Magazine*, Theosophical Society, Fall 2013. David was the co-director of Findhorn from 1970-73.

Peter Aziz: (featured in The Fairy Faith documentary) Article: *Popular Misconceptions about Fairies*. Aziz Shamanism at asiz shamanism.com/are-fairies-real/

Artistic Interpretations

Brian Froud: *Good Fairies, Bad Fairies* ~ An influential artistic and cultural interpretation informed by folklore, mythology, and traditional fairy archetypes.

Podcasts and Audio Resources

The Modern Fairy Sightings Podcast, Hosted by Jo Hickey-Hall: Interviews with individuals who share personal fairy encounters, alongside discussions of folklore, perception, and contemporary experience.

<u>Legends and Lectures Podcast</u>, Michelle Franklin: Features interviews with folklorists, historians, and researchers about fairy traditions and related topics.

<u>What the Fairy Podcast</u> ~ Hosted by Anastasia, Claire, and Emma: focuses on "cozy conversations" and practical tips for connecting with fairies in daily life, aiming to make magic accessible.

Community and Educational Gatherings

<u>Fairy Congress</u>: An annual gathering in the Pacific Northwest featuring presentations, workshops, and discussions exploring fairy folklore, mythology, and personal experience. (I have no personal experience with this, but it looked charming.)

Related Works

Fairy Faith (2000) Film: Directed by John Walker, National Film Board of Canada: A short documentary exploring contemporary beliefs and experiences with fairies, combining interviews with historical context.

<u>Mark Fox</u>: Scholar of religion and anomalous experience who has studied contemporary fairy experiences and contributed to modern academic discussion of anomalous encounters of all kinds. Featured in the documentary *Fairy Faith*. Author of *LightForms: Spiritual Encounters with Unusual Light Phenomena*

<u>Jacob Nordby</u>: *Blessed Are the Weird* ~ A reflective and affirming exploration of creativity, authenticity, and honoring one's inner knowing, especially for those who experience the world differently.

<u>David Abram</u>: *Becoming Animal* ~ A philosophical work exploring humanity's relationship with the living earth and the animate presence of the natural world.

<u>Carl Jung</u>: *The Archetypes and the Collective Unconscious* ~ This is Jung's most important work for understanding figures like fairies from a psychological and symbolic perspective.

<u>Imelda Almqvist</u>: *Sacred Art ~ A Hollow Bone for Spirit: Where Art Meets Shamanism.*

I pray that the strangely beautiful, often mysterious ways of the fairies will touch some forgotten part of you – allowing you to feel more alive, more inspired, more whole.

~ Maggie Hamilton, Author

ABOUT THE AUTHOR

Lori Sweet is an artist, writer, and teacher who explores the intersection of spirit, creativity, and everyday life. From childhood she has cultivated a lifelong devotion to inner listening, nature's wisdom, and the mystical currents of the world.

For more than forty years, Lori has guided others as a social worker, complementary healthcare practitioner, and teaching artist, supporting them in discovering their own inner wisdom and creative voice. Her work moves fluidly between imagination, contemplation, and embodied practice, inviting a gentle awareness of the sacred in daily life.

Lori lives in Harrisburg, Pennsylvania, with her husband, Tom. She enjoys writing, working in her visual arts studio, tending to her plants, playing the ancient women's frame drum, and lingering in wooded and watery places.

If you would like to learn more about the work, art, and writings of Lori Sweet, or if you have your own otherworldly story to tell, please visit her at **www.lorisweetstudios.com**

There are no endings, happy or otherwise. We all have our own stories which are just part of the one Story that binds both this world and Faerie. Sometimes we step into each others stories – perhaps just for a few minutes, perhaps for years – and then we step out of them again. But all the while the Story just goes on.

~ Charles de Lint, Author